THE A–Z OF FREE EXPRESSION

THE A-Z OF FREE EXPRESSION

Everyone has the right to freedom of opinion and expression;
this right includes freedom to hold opinions without interference
and to seek, receive and impart information and ideas
through any media and regardless of frontiers.

Article 19
Universal Declaration of Human Rights
UN 1948

INDEX
for free expression

First published 2003 by
Index on Censorship
33 Islington High Street
London N1 9LH

A CIP record for this book is available from the
British Library

ISBN 0-904286-99-1

Selected and edited by Judith Vidal-Hall
Designed by Jane Havell Associates
Cover design by Small Japanese Soldier
Cover illlustration by Dave Dragon
Printed and bound by Thanet Press, UK

Index on Censorship wishes to thank the following:

Gill Newsham for editing and coordinating; Gulliver Cragg, Henderson Mullin, Ben Owen and Natasha Schmidt for editorial support; Jane Havell for the design; Roger Thomas for proofreading; Frances Harvey, Andrew Kendle and Jason Pollard for general help, and of course special thanks to all our contributors over the past 30 years.

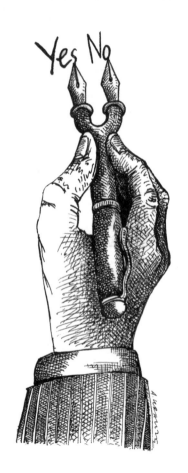

Contents

= Opinion

7

PREFACE
Ursula Owen

'We became dissidents without actually knowing how, and we found ourselves behind bars without really knowing how. We simply did certain things we had to do and that it seemed proper to do: nothing more nor less.' This was Václav Havel in *Index*, telling us that courage is a funny thing, that we don't know we have it till we've done it. A week after the piece was published in 1979, he was in jail.

It was seven years earlier that Stephen Spender had founded *Index*, responding to a plea from Soviet dissidents Pavel Litvinov and Larisa Bogarov Daniel, who were protesting against show trials in Moscow. The idea was to make public the circumstances of those who are silenced in their own countries, wherever that might be, and publish their work.

Over the past 30 years, *Index* has been there for the censored and oppressed in most parts of the globe and across the political spectrum. We tell the stories of the 'disappeared', and publish the work of banned poets. We publish prison letters, document the censoring and silencing of journalists, carry banned literary texts. And we have reported on the implacable censoring efforts of religious fundamentalists – Islamic, Jewish and Christian. Our alphabetical record of abuses and violations, in each issue of the magazine, gives a kind of ground's-eye-view of world history seen through the prism of individual names.

There were those who thought that, with the Cold War over, *Index*'s job was largely done. The world being what it is, that was unthinkable. Only the geography of censorship has changed, and sometimes not even that. What is more, as we embark on the new millennium – ideologies discredited, borders altered – new and troubling questions have surfaced, some of them challenging the primacy of free expression itself: questions around religious extremism, relative values and cultural difference, the rewriting of history, hate speech, pornography, violence on television, freedom on the internet – and, above all, around security and fear.

In the year that *Index* began to publish, Spain, Portugal and Greece were all ruled by military dictatorships, apartheid flourished in South Africa, the Soviet Empire dominated Russia and Eastern Europe, China was gripped by the Cultural Revolution, the United States was at war with Vietnam and totalitarian governments were in control in many parts of Latin America and some of the newly independent countries of Africa. In all these places, and many more, it was standard for censorship to be employed as an instrument of government. Many of these particular tyrannies have gone, only to have been replaced by others. Release from the tyranny of communism turns out not, on the whole, to have led to upsurge of creativity. We have to concern ourselves with how freedom is used as well as its suppression.

And then, on 11 September 2001, a new epoch began. The world changed utterly. In the resulting battle between security and freedom of speech, there are disturbing signs that the latter is losing out. Certainly civil liberties seem to have become a rather fragile filling between the imperatives of law and order and fears about more ruthless and desperate acts of terrorism.

We live in dangerous times. Free expression is under threat from new sources as well as old. The death toll of journalists is up, media freedom is under threat in many countries, the voices of the poor and powerless are drowned out, and governments increasingly repress media stories on corruption. The right to freedom of expression and access to information has rarely been needed more. Stephen Spender, the founder of *Index*, once said that 'the opposite of censorship is self-expression, which is literature,' and from the beginning *Index* ranged itself on the side of the scribblers. That remains our task. We'll continue to defend, everywhere, the right of people to tell their stories, and the right of the imagination to flourish.

A NEW MAP OF CENSORSHIP
Ronald Dworkin

Is freedom of speech a universal human right? Or is it, after all, just one value among others, a value cherished by middle-class intellectuals in Western democracies, but one that other cultures, drawing on different traditions, might well reject as unsuitable for them, and that radical groups within those Western democracies might well challenge as no longer central even there?

Index was founded in the first conviction: that freedom of speech, along with the allied freedoms of conscience and religion, are fundamental human rights that the world community has a responsibility to guard. But that strong conviction is suddenly challenged not only by freedom's oldest enemies – the despots and ruling thieves who fear it – but also by new enemies who claim to speak for justice not tyranny, and who point to other values we respect, including self-determination, equality, and freedom from racial hatred and prejudice, as reasons why the right of free speech should now be demoted to a much lower grade of urgency and importance.

In part, this new hostility reflects reluctance to impose Western values on alien cultures. Free speech may be important within our own secular traditions, some critics say, but it would make no sense to graft it on to very different styles of life. We cannot reasonably ask peoples whose entire social structure and sense of national identity are based on the supreme authority of a particular religion to permit what they believe to be ridicule of that religion within their own borders.

How can we expect people who are committed to a particular faith, as a value transcending all others, to tolerate its open desecration?

Other critics insist that free speech is overvalued even within Western democracies, and particularly within the USA. When the Supreme Court ruled, in the Skokie case, that the Constitution's First Amendment protected neo-Nazis who wanted to carry swastikas through a town of Holocaust survivors in Illinois, many people of good will wonder how justice could require people to accept such a grotesque insult. In the decades since the Skokie decision, moreover, Americans have become even more aware of the malign, chilling force of hate-speech and hate-gesture. That kind of speech seems particularly odious in universities, where it has been directed against women and minority students and fuelled by a backlash against the affirmative-action and other special recruiting programmes such universities adopted to increase the number of such students.

Officials at some of these universities have adopted 'speech codes' to prohibit remarks that are sexist or derogatory of a particular race or religion or sexual orientation; they defend that apparent violation of freedom of speech by insisting that the regulations are necessary to protect the dignity and equal status of all students. Some speech code supporters have taken the opportunity not just to argue for an exception to free speech, however, but to deny its importance in principle. They say that though the right of free speech has been much prized by liberal writers who profit from it, it has proved of little value to the poor and disadvantaged, and has often acted as an excuse for their oppression. One such critic, Stanley Fish, declared that: 'There's no such thing as free speech, and a good thing too.'

But the strongest new attack on freedom of speech, within democracies, has been organised by those feminists who are anxious to outlaw pornography or to make its publishers liable for punitive damages if a rapist or other criminal convinces a jury that pornography made him act as he did. They say that pornography contributes to a general cultural environment in which women are treated only as sexual devices, and subordinated to men in every way. One such American feminist, Catharine MacKinnon, is contemptuous of the objection that such censorship violates an important right; she says that Americans elevate freedom of speech to an absurd level of importance, and that more sensible people, in other parts of the worlds, recognise that it is to be tolerated only so long as it does not jeopardise more important goals.

Even Tom Stoppard, a distinguished and long-standing patron of *Index*, has joined in this recent demotion of free speech. Speaking at an anniversary of Khomeini's hideous fatwa against Salman Rushdie, Stoppard said that though it was of course outrageous for Iran's priests to suppose that they had a right to order a murder in Britain, it was nevertheless a mistake to regard freedom of speech as a 'fundamental' human right. 'The proscription of writing which seeks to incite race hatred sits as comfortably in the Western liberal conscience', he said, 'as the proscription against falsely shouting FIRE! in a crowded theatre.'

These are all thoughtful opinions that will strike many people as reasonable. They signal, just for that reason, a new and particularly dangerous threat to free speech, for we are more likely to relax our defence of that freedom when its betrayers are foreign, or when the speech in question seems worthless or even vile. But if we do, then the principle is inevitably weakened, not just in such cases but generally. So we must try to abstract from the particular challenges to free speech that now dominate the argument, and to return to the wider question I began by asking. Is free speech a universal human right, a right so important that we must work to secure it even in nations where it is unfamiliar and alien? Is it so important that we must tolerate, in its name, despicable and harmful speech in our own society?

I do not mean, by posing that last question, to agree that bad speech has had the malign consequences that have recently been claimed for it. Many of those claims are inflated and some are absurd. But if free speech really is as fundamental as many of its defenders have supposed in the past, we must protect it even if it does have bad consequences, and we must be prepared to explain why. We must explain this, moreover, bearing in mind everything that, if we are right, must be tolerated. It may seem easy to defend the rights to investigative reporters exposing corruption or serious novelists exploring literary and intellectual boundaries. But free speech, if it is a universal right, also protects pornographers hawking pictures of naked women with their legs spread, and bigots sporting swastikas or white hoods and selling hatred.

We must start by recognising that the most famous and honoured defence of free speech – John Stuart Mill's argument *On Liberty* – cannot support a right with that scope. Mill said that we should tolerate even the speech we hate because truth is most likely to emerge in a free intellectual combat from which no idea has been excluded. People with passionate religious convictions think they already know the truth, however, and they can hardly be expected to have more confidence in Mill's doubtful epistemology than in their own bibles. Nor could Mill's optimism justify, even to us, tolerating everything that those who believe free speech is a basic human right insist should be tolerated. Pornographic images hardly supply 'ideas' to any market place of thought, and history gives us little reason for expecting racist speech to contribute to its own refutation.

If freedom of speech is a basic right, this must be so not in virtue of instrumental arguments, like Mill's, which suppose that liberty is important because of its consequences. It must be so for reasons of basic principle. We can find that basic principle, moreover. We can find it in a condition of human dignity: it is illegitimate for governments to impose a collective or official decision on dissenting individuals, using the coercive powers of the state, unless that decision has been taken in a manner that respects each individual's status as a free and equal member of the community. People who believe in democracy think that it is fair to use the police power to enforce the law if the law has been adopted through democratic political procedures that express the majority's will. But though majoritarian procedures may be a necessary condition of political legitimacy, they are not a sufficient condition. Fair democracy requires what we might call a democratic background: it requires, for example, that every competent adult have a vote in deciding what the majority's will is. And it requires, further, that each citizen have not just a vote but a voice: a majority decision is not fair unless everyone has had a fair opportunity to express his or her attitudes or opinions or fears or tastes or presuppositions or prejudices or ideals, not just in the hope of influencing others, though that hope is crucially important, but also just to confirm his or her standing as a responsible agent in, rather than a passive victim of, collective action. The majority has no right to impose its will on someone who is forbidden to raise a voice in protest or argument or objection before the decision is taken.

That is not the only reason for insisting on freedom of speech as a condition of political legitimacy, but it is a central one. It may be objected that in most democracies that right now has little value for many citizens: ordinary people, with no access to great newspapers or television broadcasts, have little chance to be heard. That is a genuine problem; it may be that genuine free speech requires more than just freedom from legal censorship. But that is hardly an excuse for denying at least that freedom and the dignity it confirms: we must try to find other ways of providing those without money or influence a real chance to make their voices heard.

This argument entails a great deal more than just that governments may not censor formal political speeches or writing. A community's legislation and policy are determined more by its moral and cultural environment – the mix of its people's opinions, prejudices, tastes and attitudes – than by editorial columns or party political broadcasts or stump political speeches. It is as unfair to impose a collective decision on someone who has not been allowed to contribute to that moral environment, by expressing his political or social convictions or tastes or prejudices informally, as on someone whose pamphlets against the decision were destroyed by the police. This is true no matter how offensive the majority takes these convictions or tastes or prejudices to be, or how reasonable its objection is.

The temptation may be near overwhelming to make exceptions to that principle – to declare that people have no right to pour the filth of pornography or race-hatred into the culture in which we all must live. But we cannot do that without forfeiting our moral title to force such people to bow to

the collective judgements that do make their way into the statute books. We may and must protect women and homosexuals and members of minority groups from specific and damaging consequences of sexism, intolerance and racism. We must protect them against unfairness and inequality in employment or education or housing or the criminal process, for example, and we may adopt laws to achieve that protection. But we must not try to intervene further upstream, by forbidding any expression of the attitudes or prejudices that we think nourish such unfairness or inequality, because if we intervene too soon in the process through which collective opinion is formed, we spoil the only democratic justification we have for insisting that everyone obey these laws, even those who hate and resent them.

Someone might now object that my argument shows, at most, only that free speech is essential to a democracy, and therefore does not show that it is a universal human right that may properly be claimed even in non-democratic societies. We may want to reply, to that objection, that democracy is itself a universal human right, and that non-democratic societies are tyrannies. But we need not rely on that claim, because we can distinguish democracy, as a form of political organisation, from the more basic obligation of government to treat all those subject to its dominion with equal concern, as all people whose lives matter. That plainly is a basic human right; and many of the more detailed human rights we all recognise flow from it. And so does a right of free speech. Even in a country ruled by prophets or generals in which ordinary citizens have no real vote, these citizens must nevertheless have the right to speak out, to cry for the attention or to buy the ear of those who will decide their fates, or simply to bear witness, out of self-respect if nothing else, to what they believe to be wicked or unfair. A government that deems them too corrupt or debased or ignoble even to be heard, except on penalty of death or jail, can hardly pretend that it counts their interests as part of its own.

It is tempting to think that even if some liberty of speech must be counted a universal right, this right cannot be absolute; that those whose opinions are too threatening or base or contrary to the moral or religious consensus have forfeited any right to the concern on which the right rests. But such a reservation would destroy the principle: it would leave room only for the pointless grant of protection for ideas or tastes or prejudices that those in power approve, or in any case do not fear. We might have the power to silence those we despise, but it would be at the cost of political legitimacy, which is more important than they are.

Any such reservation would also be dangerous. War is always a bad time for free speech, because political and social pressures chill any genuine criticism of or even debate about government's security and military measures. Following the catastrophe in New York on 11 September 2001, the Bush administration adopted new legislation and policies defining the crime of terrorism in breathtakingly broad terms, permitting preventive detention of suspected terrorists, allowing conversations between them and their lawyers to be monitored, and substantially broadening surveillance powers. But few of the organisations or politicians who have traditionally defended civil liberties spoke out in protest, and those who did were told by the attorney general that they were aiding terrorists themselves.

Following the military success in Afghanistan, President Bush has floated a proposal to carry the war against terrorism to other nations as well, including Iraq, North Korea and Iran, countries he declared to form an 'axis of evil'. The public debate over the wisdom and feasibility of this frightening and portentous plan should be full and free. But when the Democratic Senate Majority Leader, Tom Daschle, questioned the plan in a tentative way, the Republican Minority Leader, Senator Trent Lott, rounded on him. 'How dare Senator Daschle criticise President Bush while we are fighting our war on terrorism?' he declared. That is politics, of course, but it is dangerous politics. It threatens to weaken democracy just when it needs to be strong.

Principle is indivisible, and we try to divide it at our peril. When we compromise on freedom because we think our immediate goals more important, we are likely to find that the power to exploit the compromise is not in our own hands after all, but in those of fanatical priests armed with fatwas and fanatical moralists with their own brand of hate.

ACADEMIC FREEDOM

ACCESS TO INFORMATION

ADVERTISING

ANTI-SEMITISM

ARMS

ART

ARTICLE 19

ASYLUM

ACADEMIC FREEDOM

♦ Freedom must go hand in hand with being better informed and understanding more and better.

♦ The new theology that has gained currency in the seminaries and in the religious and academic community is an auspicious development.

♦ They thought that a single jurist could bring *fiqh* (jurisprudence) to life, whereas the thing that can lead to dynamism in *fiqh* is the discipline of theology. And, since the discipline of theology has been shut down here for centuries, our *fiqh* has gone stale as well.

♦ What surprises me most is my critics' accusation that I'm disturbing the public. I'm happy to be accused of the same crime as Socrates. They tried and sentenced him on the charge of disturbing the minds of Athens' youths.

Abdol Karim Soroush on Iran 2002

♦ Twenty-five% of the 4,000 people executed or tortured to death in Iraq between 1968 and 1981 were academics.

Nasreddine Hajjaj 1981

♦ Odd though it may appear, many national and European cultural and research institutions, including especially those funded from the EU and the European Science Foundation, regard Israel as a European state for the purposes of awarding grants and contracts. (No other Middle Eastern state is so regarded.) Would it not, therefore, be timely if at both national and European level a moratorium was called upon any further such support unless and until Israel abides by UN resolutions and opens serious peace negotiations with the Palestinians.

Hilary and Steven Rose 2002

♦ The most common question put to me was: why pick on Israel when so many other, more horrible things are happening in the world? What about the Russian treatment of Chechnya or the Chinese treatment of Tibet? . . . Israeli intellectuals are much more likely to be in a position to influence the political process in their own country than are Russian or Chinese intellectuals in theirs.

♦ By a process known as 'affiliation bias', scientists consciously or unconsciously tailor their published findings to the wishes of their paymasters, whether they be the tobacco or the food industries, civil servants making procurements for national defence or pharmaceutical companies.

♦ Influences flow both ways and the impact of scientists on society can also be very considerable. If their funding is threatened by the actions of their own government, their initial response will certainly be to protest volubly that they have nothing to do with political decisions, but then they can start to exert the real influence they do possess.

♦ I have felt ambivalence about the recommended moratorium on funding for Israeli academic institutions because it does, indeed, run counter to the ideals – if not the practice – of our profession. But the debate needs to be treated with proper seriousness.

Patrick Bateson on boycotts 2002

ACCESS TO INFORMATION

♦ And for those of us who are as concerned about the right to read what we choose as the right to write what we choose, it is alarming that the business of demanding bans on whatever ideas get up people's noses is getting to be respectable. It's getting to be *cool*.

Salman Rushdie on the US 1996

♦ The denial of information is, of course, a form of censorship. A public who knows nothing is not free to criticise or denounce injustice. However, the newly suggested Official Secrets reform goes further than preserving secrecy. It might well act as a protection for the most serious crimes, including fraud and murder, provided that such crimes are committed by a government servant in what he might conceive, however wrongheadedly, to be the exercise of his duties.

John Mortimer on the UK 1988

ADVERTISING

♦ When advertisers come to foot an appreciable proportion of overall media costs, they come to dominate that medium's workaday self-conciousness, which in turn places new pressures and limits upon that medium's relationship with its audience.

Dan Schiller 1997

♦ The advertising industry has agreed, as a matter of self-interest, to regulate itself. Governments and international bodies have considered it desirable to restrict advertisements of such products as tobacco, alcohol and firearms.

♦ The European Court of Human Rights has held that information of a commercial nature is protected by Article 10 of the European Convention on Human Rights, but has granted governments a wider measure of freedom to restrict commercial speech than other forms of expression.

♦ The federal court of Germany stopped an advertising campaign by the Italian clothing company Benetton in 1995, holding that the portrayal of an oil-covered duck, child labour in the Third World, and unclothed parts of the human body bearing the stamp 'HIV positive' went beyond prescribed acceptable limits; it was particularly objectionable to 'brand' Aids sufferers as if they were excluded from human society.

♦ In Uganda during 1996, the senior presidential adviser on the media and public relations warned opposition newspapers that governments all over the world 'have the power to withdraw favours from papers that undermine them'. This is particularly serious in countries where the majority of staple industries are publicly owned, and the press almost entirely dependent on advertising for its survival.

Candelaria van Strien-Reney *Censorship: A World Encyclopaedia*
(Fitzroy Dearborn, UK 2001)

♦ An advertisement sponsored by the black newspaper *The Voice* depicting the situation of blacks in Britain was rejected by the

Independent Television Companies Association as being 'too politically controversial'.

Index archive 1983

ANTI-SEMITISM

♦ European anti-semitism would appear to be some sort of ineradicable cultural stain.

Nicholas Fraser 2001

♦ Anti-semitism is not within the category of thought which must be protected by the right to free opinion.

Jean-Paul Sartre 1955, quoted by Nicholas Fraser 2001

♦ It's undeniable that virtually every Pole is bound to encounter anti-Semitism in some form, somewhere, even if he has never actually met a Jew.

Rafal Pankowski 2000

ARMS

♦ A well regulated Militia, being necessary to the security of a free state, the right of the people to keep and bear Arms, shall not be infringed.

Second Amendment US Constitution 1791

♦ There have been very few 'whistleblowers' from within the arms-sales business, chiefly because of the character of the people who go into it in the first place. And without such whistleblowers, the media need far greater resources and motivation if they are to provide their own oversight of the arms trade.

♦ The involvement of the media, whether in the developing or the developed world, is essential to any pressure to restrict the arms trade. For arms selling still needs secrecy to protect it: the most irresponsible acts of governments, like the US Irangate conspiracy, or the European sales to Iraq, would never have been allowed if they had been submitted to Parliament or Congress. And the media, once motivated and equipped, can do much to increase disclosure and mobilise public opinion.

♦ The media, with their own traditional bias towards military sources and war reporting, are unlikely to mobilise themselves as effective monitors of arms sales without external pressure. Only a major change in the political scene, together with more effective institutions dedicated to arms control, are likely to make newspapers and television as interested in preventing wars as they are in reporting them.

Anthony Sampson 1991

ART

♦ 'Everyone has the right freely to participate in the cultural life of the community, to enjoy the arts and to share in scientific advancement and its benefits.'

Universal Declaration of Human Rights Article 27

♦ In the art world today, the first amendment is routinely invoked to justify or protect objects and behaviour whose entire raison d'être is to shock and discommode.

♦ Any where and everywhere in American society the foulest possible language, the most graphic images of sexual congress and sexual perversion, the most inflammatory speech ridiculing political and religious leaders abounds.

♦ The idea that art – or any other form of expression, for that matter – is censored in the US today is preposterous.

Roger Kimball 1996

♦ Both the most modern and most ancient elements in Arabic culture tend to predispose artists to resist the advance of fundamentalism in the contemporary visual arts.

Edward Lucie-Smith 1997

♦ In the United States, the 1980s and 1990s saw a series of running battles between artists and the US art world in general, and conservative politicians often allied to the Christian right. Mostly these battles were to do with sex and representations of sexuality but religion also played a part.

♦ The history of art in the West (but not exclusively in the West) is a long history of struggle for the right to free expression, and the 'culture wars' that raged through America in the 1980s concerned the right of artists, such as Robert Mapplethorpe, to freedom of expression within a supposedly individualist liberal culture. It is therefore paradoxical that feminists, who have fought so long for the right to a voice of their own, have been complicit in the censorship of works of which they disapprove. For example, at one American university women objected to the display of a Goya painting, the *Naked Maja*, on the grounds that it was offensive to women.

Elizabeth Wilson 2000

ARTICLE 19

♦ 'Everyone has the right to freedom of opinion and expression; this right includes freedom to hold opinions without interference and to seek, receive and impart information and ideas through any media and regardless of frontiers.'

Universal Declaration of Human Rights

♦ At its half-century mark, Article 19 remains more poetry than reality.

Bill Orme 1998

ASYLUM

♦ The success of the *Daily Mail* in imposing its views of asylum seekers on a government allegedly proud of its youthfulness and fresh-mindedness is an indication that these ideas are here to stay.

Nicholas Fraser on the UK 2001

♦ Asylum seekers have never been popular but in the last ten years or so, their 'image problem' – in a world where image marketing is paramount – has got very much worse. Their image is tarnished by their association with illegality, racketeering and disregard for sovereign borders.

♦ Paragraph 1, Article 31 of the 1951 Convention Relating to the Status of Refugees recognises that they may be obliged to use illicit means of entry into a safe country and requires that host countries 'shall not impose penalties' on that account.

♦ We have also forgotten that, historically, asylum seekers have often had to lie and dissimulate in order to get to a safe country – an amnesia that allows us to make their journeys even more dangerous than they might be.

Jeremy Harding on the UK 2000

BANNING

BLASPHEMY

BODIES

BOOKS

BURNING

BANNING

♦ We can only prohibit that which we can name.

George Steiner, quoted by Alberto Manguel 1996

♦ The bannings of the far right are as demeaning as the prosecution of internet service providers for harbouring peddlers of Nazi memorabilia.

Nicholas Fraser 2001

♦ It was no coincidence that when Manuel Puig's *La traición de Rita Hayworth* (Betrayed by Rita Hayworth) appeared in 1968, at the beginning of the military dictatorship in Argentina, it was quickly banned. The mild, somewhat autobiographical tale offended not only the official sensibility, but also the sensibility of the common reader: in General Villegas, Puig's home town, the book was burned by the townspeople in the public square. What was offensive to the public was that a homosexual lifestyle could be described as happy, or at least not unhappier than that of other small-town lives.

Alberto Manguel 1995

♦ If we ban whatever offends any group in our diverse society, we will soon have no art, no culture, no humour, no satire. Satire is by its nature offensive. So is much art and political discourse. The value of these expressions far outweighs their risk.

Erica Jong 1995

♦ The Turkish ban on all things Kurdish – language, culture, simply the mention of the word even in the Turkish language – resulted in widespread hardship for all Kurds and drove hundreds of thousands of them into exile. Yet the people and the identity survive, articulated nowhere more than in the songs 'ancient and modern' of their homeland.

Gill Newsham 2002

♦ This seems a puzzling and perhaps disturbing contradiction: one of the world's most liberal democracies [Germany] banning political books and hate speech in the interests of preserving itself as a liberal democracy.

Paul Oppenheimer 1998

♦ The five-volume *Cities of Salt* by exiled Saudi novelist Abdelrahan Munif – savage, surreal and satirical – angered the [Saudi] royal family. He was deprived of his nationality and banned from ever returning to the country. His books became delicious contraband, circulating everywhere – including the royal palace.

Tariq Ali 2001

BLASPHEMY

♦ Every publication is said to be blasphemous which contains any contemptuous, reviling, scurrilous or ludicrous matter relating to God, Jesus Christ, or the Bible, or the formularies of the Church of England as by law established. It is not blasphemous to speak or publish opinions hostile to the Christian religion, or to deny the existence of God, if the publication is couched in decent and temperate language. The test to be applied is as to the manner in which the doctrines are advocated and not as to the substance of the doctrines themselves'

Stephen's Digest of the Criminal Law 9th edition 1950

♦ In the early 1990s the British Board of Film Classification ruled that Nigel Wingrove's video film *Visions of Ecstasy* could not be shown because its subject matter – 'the mingling of religious ecstasy and sexual passion, depicting a sexual attraction to Christ on the part of St Theresa – might have been blasphemous' and thus, still, illegal.

♦ Blasphemy has now been reduced to 'giving offence' to those of a religious persuasion, and the law cannot be usefully employed to protect the latter from such 'insults'. Throughout the twentieth century, active Christians in most countries have campaigned particularly against films that have caused them hurt – *The Miracle, The Life of Brian, The Last Temptation of Christ,* and many others. They have sometimes persuaded film censors to make cuts, but in no case have they managed to have the film banned, with the partial exception of *Visions of Ecstasy.*

♦ The *fatwa* declared against Salman Rushdie and his publishers in 1989 introduced for the first time an international and multicultural dimension to the censorship of blasphemy. By 1949 Lord Denning, Master of the Rolls, was of the view that 'there is no such danger to society and the offence of blasphemy is a dead letter'. The law has nevertheless stayed in place, but is now used hardly at all.

David Nash *Censorship: A World Encyclopaedia*

♦ Every blasphemy law, every book-burning, every witch-hunt of the right or left, has been defended on the same ground: that it protects fundamental values from desecration.

Ronald Dworkin 1995

BODIES

♦ Considering the amount of clamour it's raised, one of the anti-choice movement's greatest triumphs is paradoxical: it has wrought a near-total public silence on abortion in any discussion of teen sex.

Judith Levine on the US 2000

♦ Alongside the official abortions demanded by the state are those undertaken secretly and voluntarily by women when they find out that they are carrying a female foetus.

Naila Kabeer on China 1995

♦ When I was asked how an anti-abortionist could favour the death penalty, the question might as easily have been put the other way: how can a pro-abortionist, or a pro-euthanasist, condemn the death penalty?

♦ It seems as paradoxical that those who support choice in abortion and euthanasia are most vehement in their opposition to the death penalty for especially heinous murder.

♦ Anyone who has observed a late abortion – as I have – can see that the foetus puts up a fight to survive, shrinking away from the lethal needle that extracts the amniotic fluid. If it had a choice, the foetus signals that it would choose to live.

♦ I have never felt the same about *Anna Karenina* since interviewing a train driver who had had a suicide under the wheels of his engine.

♦ Only the notion that the spark of human life is somehow divine and must be respected as such, will, in the final analysis, sustain the pro-life argument.

Mary Kenny 2002

♦ The hundreds of death announcements in the daily papers read only: 'untimely death after a short illness'. HIV and Aids are associated with prostitution, so to admit infection is to bring shame on the family. The very word Aids is so taboo that people avoid it, preferring to say '*iyoyo*' (that thing over there). In Zimbabwe several government ministers are thought to have died from the disease but none announced it publicly while alive, and even after their deaths it was kept a secret. Women all over the country are censoring other female members of their families, under family pressure to keep silent. Zimbabwean men generally censor themselves by not declaring their infected status.

Kim Normanton 2000

♦ I have a job as an Aids counsellor. It really is a big problem getting people to talk about it here in Zimbabwe. It is such a great taboo. My job involves counselling Aids orphans. Women should stand up and tell their children their father died of this disease, but they'd rather sweep it under the carpet, even if it means their children will die of the same thing.

Stembiso on Zimbabwe 2000

BOOKS

♦ Legend has it that when the conqueror Amr ibn al-As entered
Alexandria in 642, he ordered Caliph Umar I to set fire to the library's
books.

♦ In 1526, the soldiers of the Turkish army set fire to the Great Corvina
Library, founded by Matthias Corvinus and said to be one of the jewels
of the Hungarian crown. Almost three centuries later, in 1806, their
descendants emulated them by burning the extraordinary Fatimid Library
in Cairo, containing over 100,000 volumes dating back to the early
Middle Ages.

Alberto Manguel 1999

♦ But all around the walls there are bookcases. They're filled with books. Books and books and books, right out in plain view, no locks, no boxes. No wonder we can't come in here. It's an oasis of the forbidden. I try not to stare.

Margaret Atwood, quoted by Alberto Manguel 1999

♦ There also seems to be a belief in China that if the number of copies of a particular book is limited in some way its impact will also remain thus limited. A maximum of 50,000 copies may be printed of any one book, and they can only be distributed through the Xinhua bookstore. Publishers are also instructed to limit the number of such books on their lists each year.

Urvashi Butalia 1996

BURNING

♦ One day, in the illustrious nation of Panduria, a suspicion crept into the minds of top officials: that books contained opinions hostile to military prestige. . . . A commission of inquiry was set up under General Fedina, a severe and scrupulous official.

One bright morning the commission finally left the library and went to report to the chief of staff; and General Fedina illustrated the results of the inquiry before an assembly of the General Staff. His speech was a kind of compendium of human history in which all those ideas considered beyond discussion by the right-minded folk of Panduria were attacked, in which the ruling classes were declared responsible for the nation's misfortunes, and the people exalted as the heroic victims of mistaken policies and unnecessary wars.

Italo Calvino on Italy 1996

♦ On 14 January 1989, Muslims in Bradford, Yorkshire, burned a copy of *The Satanic Verses*, in order to draw attention to their grievances.

Fiction, Fact and the Fatwa: A Chronology of Censorship (Article 19, 1992)

♦ *We're* book-burners, too. We read the books and burnt them, afraid they'd be found. Better to keep it in the old heads, where no one can see it or suspect it. We are all bits and pieces of history and literature and international law. Byron, Tom Paine, Machiavelli or Christ, it's here.

Ray Bradbury *Fahrenheit 451* 1953, quoted in *Index* 1999

♦ In Uruguay, the inquisitors have updated themselves. Strange mixture of the Middle Ages and the capitalist concept of business. The military don't burn books any more: they sell them to the paper manufacturers.

Eduardo Galeano 1978

♦ In memoirs and autobiographies, such as Sean O'Faolain's and the poet Austin Clarke's, the greater book-burners were their mothers.

Mary Kenny 2000

C

CAPITAL PUNISHMENT

CENSORSHIP

CHILDREN

CORRUPTION

CAPITAL PUNISHMENT

♦ The USA is one of only four countries in the world – Pakistan, Yemen and Saudi Arabia are the others – that regularly sentence juveniles, those under the age of 18 when their crime was committed, to death.

♦ China heads the league of countries with gruesome practices and, with well over 1,500 people executed every year, far exceeds all other places for numbers.

♦ Far less numerous but just as shocking are the beheadings handed down under *sharia* law in Saudi Arabia for apostasy, certain acts of sabotage, treason or conspiracy against the state, some sexual offences and robbery with violence.

♦ Public executions continue in Nigeria, where, on 2 August 1994, 38 prisoners were shot by a firing squad before a crowd of 20,000 people in Enugu, in the southeast.

Caroline Moorehead 1995

♦ In America, capital punishment is *so* popular that even the denizens of death row support it. No comparable nation has such a lurid gun-club following, or such an intimate acquaintance with domestic and civil homicide.

♦ With the exception of Japan, no other advanced industrial country executes people any more, but then no other 'advanced industrial country' is so close to the memory of frontier justice.

Christopher Hitchens 1995

♦ I believe the death penalty to be an effective means of protecting the public from cold-blooded killers who have no respect for innocent lives.

Gov. William F Weld 1995

♦ Survey research year after year reports a large and stable majority, about 80–85% of the adult population regardless of age, gender, race, political party or socio-economic class, in favour of executions.

♦ Recent academic research confirms the results of earlier investigations in showing no discernible benefits from the death penalty.

Hugo Bedau on the US 1995

♦ Capital cases cost at least an extra US$2.16 million per execution, compared with what tax payers would have spent if defendants were tried without the death penalty and sentenced to life in prison. Applying these figures on a national level implies that over US$200 million was spent just for US executions in the past three years. Yet the national concern about crime indicates that few feel safer for the expense.

Richard Dieter 1995

♦ Americans are well aware that the death penalty is biased by class and race; a 1991 Gallup Poll found that 45% of a national sample agreed with the statement: 'A black person is more likely than a white person to receive the death penalty for the same crime.' Sixty per cent believed that the poor were more likely than the rich to be condemned to death for the same crime.

Michael L Radelet 1995

CENSORSHIP

♦ Some time in 1941, Jorge Luis Borges noted that in a riddle whose subject is chess, the only word that cannot be mentioned is precisely the word 'chess'. 'To *always* omit a word, to make use of inept metaphors and self-evident paraphrases,' writes Borges, 'is perhaps the most emphatic way of pointing it out.' The paradoxical ability of censorship is that, in its efforts to suppress, it highlights that which it wishes to condemn: it draws attention to clearings of silence in the tangles of our languages and our literatures. Spanish has an idiom, 'it shines through its absence', that precisely describes censorship's innermost failure.

Alberto Manguel 1995

♦ The history of censorship is to some extent the history of suppressing and controlling what people see, based on elitist fears of mass access.

Amy Adler 1996

♦ I know how strong the case for censorship seems in Germany now; I know that decent people are impatient with abstract principles when they see hoodlums with pseudo-swastikas pretending that the most monumental, cold-blooded genocide ever was the invention of its victims. The hoodlums remind us of what we often forget: the high, sometimes nearly unbearable, cost of freedom.

Ronald Dworkin 1995

♦ It has always seemed to me that limits of censorship are defined by two famous quotations: Voltaire's 'I disagree with everything you say – but will fight to the death for your right to say it' and Chief Justice Holmes's: 'Freedom of speech does not include the liberty to shout FIRE! in a crowded theatre.' In real life, one must attempt to steer a course between these two extremes. Thus I can tolerate astrologers purveying their (usually) harmless nonsense, but not anti-Semites and neo-Nazis hawking their poison.

♦ What I am saying is that the debate about the free flow of information which has been going on for so many years will soon be settled – by engineers, not politicians. (Just as physicists, not generals, have now determined the nature of war.) Consider what this means. No government will be able to conceal, at least for very long, evidence of crimes or atrocities – even from its own people. The very existence of the myriads of new information channels, operating in real time and across all frontiers, will be a powerful influence for civilised behaviour. If you are arranging a massacre, it will be useless to shoot the cameraman who has so inconveniently appeared on the scene. His pictures will already be safe in the studio 5,000 kilometres away; and his final image may hang you.

♦ Exposures of scandals or political abuses – especially by visiting TV teams who go home and make rude documentaries – can be painful but also very valuable. Many a ruler might still be in power today, or even alive, had he known what was really happening in his own country. A wise statesman once said: 'A free press can give you hell; but it can save your skin.' To sum up: as this century draws to a close, it looks as if all the old arguments about censorship will be made obsolete by wide-band, person-to-person communications. When you can download anything and everything 'in the privacy of your own home', as certain notorious advertisements used to say, not even entire armies of Thought Police will be able to do anything about it.

♦ The real challenge now facing us through the internet and the world wide web is not quality but sheer quantity. How will we find anything – and not merely our favourite porn – in the overwhelming cyberbabble of billions of humans and trillions of computers, all chattering simultaneously? I don't know the answer: and I have a horrible feeling that there may not be one.

Arthur C Clarke 1995

♦ It only takes a little refinement to render overt censorship unnecessary: it can be achieved without anyone being any the wiser.

Anneliese Rohrer 2001

♦ Censorship was practised on the broadest possible basis: it not only shielded people from everything that was ideologically suspect, from everything new and potentially disturbing; it also protected them from the worst trash.

Ivan Klíma on Eastern Europe 1994

♦ Censorship in India is so strict under Indira Gandhi that newspapers were no longer allowed to print extracts from speeches by Nehru, Gandhi or Tagore which relate to freedom or touch upon the kind of emergency measures then being introduced.

Jesse Banfield 1975

♦ The big media have been very intimidated – who decided no gruesome pictures of the World Trade Centre site were to be published anywhere? I don't think there was any directive but there was an extraordinary consensus, a kind of self-censorship by media executives who concluded that these images would be too demoralising for the country.

Susan Sontag 2002

♦ Censorship is introduced by those who fear public opinion, the very existence of censorship is a sign that oppositional thought is alive and cannot be eradicated – that alongside the ruling bureaucratic 'party' there is also a de facto democratic party.

Harvey J Kaye 1995

♦ I had always believed banishment from one's own country to be the most outrageous form of censorship that could be inflicted on any person; probably second only to execution.

♦ Because almost everybody suffered some form of censorship or self-censorship in Banda's Malawi we were forced to find alternative strategies for survival; alternative metaphors for the expression of our feelings and ideas. Writing was only one form of therapy; most of us did not write to seek fame or readership; we wrote to survive spiritually and to keep our sanity.

Jack Mapanje on Malawi 1997

♦ Censorship first occurs when a writer revises and improves a text. The next, still tolerable censorship is 'editing', when author and editor argue the toss.

♦ Sometimes censorship begins at home. Sometimes those who practise it are the writers who most vigorously champion the freedoms they privately curtail.

Michael Schmidt 1997

♦ But what about the invisible cages? In what official report or opposition document do the prisoners of fear figure? Fear of losing one's job, fear of not finding one; fear of speaking, fear of hearing, fear of reading. In the country of silence, a brightness in the eyes can send one to a concentration camp. A functionary doesn't have to be sacked: it's sufficient to let him know that he can be removed without notice and that he'll never get another job. Censorship triumphs when every citizen becomes the implacable censor of his own words and actions.

♦ Dictatorship makes its prisons from barracks, police stations, abandoned carriages, disused ships. And what it does with everyone's house, isn't that the same thing?

Eduardo Galeano on Uruguay 1978

♦ What are the effects of total censorship? Obviously, the absence of information and the presence of lies. During Mr Bhutto's campaign of genocide in Baluchistan, the news media remained silent. Officially, Baluchistan was at peace. Those who died, died unofficial deaths. It must have comforted them to know that the State's truth declared them all to be alive. Another example: you will not find the involvement of Pakistan's military rulers with the booming heroin industry much discussed in the country's news media. Yet this is what underlies General Zia's concern for the lot of the Afghan refugees. It is Afghan free enterprise that runs the Pakistan heroin business, and they have had the good sense to make sure that they make the army rich as well as themselves. How fortunate that the Quran does not mention anything about the ethics of heroin pushing.

♦ But the worst, most insidious effect of censorship is that, in the end, it can deaden the imagination of the people. Where there is no debate, it is hard to go on remembering, every day, that there is a suppressed side to every argument. It becomes almost impossible to conceive of what the suppressed things might be. It becomes easy to think that what has been suppressed was valueless anyway, or so dangerous that it needed to be suppressed. And then the victory of the censor is total. The anti-Gandhi letter-writer who recommended narrow-mindedness as a national virtue is one such casualty of censorship; he loves Big Brother – or *Burra Bhai*, perhaps.

Salman Rushdie 1983

♦ The progress of culture is not helped by monstrous censorship, which bans all truthful and courageous words, sentences, articles or ideas. It censors what was written by pens soaked in truth. And after all, words, in order to be alive, have to be truthful.

Jerzy Popieuszko 1985

♦ I mention all this only because I think that your latest idea – to register all typewriters in the country – requires a little more elaboration. Allow me therefore to discuss this interesting measure and to make a few suggestions as to how it could be improved. First of all, it is absolutely essential also to register chalks, pens, crayons, pencils, brushes, as well as ink, varnishes and sprays (insofar as these are obtainable in your country), and other material such as paper, note-pads and exercise-books. And talking about paper, you mustn't forget wrapping and toilet paper. Also all kinds of material used to cut out, stick on or otherwise position letters of the alphabet. I am referring to newspapers, sacks, textiles, scissors, glues, drawing pins, needles, pins and nails.

Ivan Kraus on Romania 1985

♦ Robert Louis Stevenson – a firm believer in the transcendent reality of fiction – found himself censored by the same sociopathic culture which had, for centuries, allowed Britons to commit genocide at home and abroad. When he wrote 'The Beach of Falesa' he produced a wonderful fable of squalor, violence, immorality and waste. It was not released in an unexpurgated form until almost 100 years after its initial publication because of its 'profanity'.

AL Kennedy 2002

♦ A woman's life is censored from start to finish, and if not censored then severely edited.

Anon, Indian woman writer 2002

♦ Scissors to cut with, a needle and thread to sew my lips with. If I write my subconscious the earth will be covered with paper.

Anamika, Indian woman writer 2002

♦ Censorship often takes place within the home, where manuscripts may be destroyed, suppressed or altered by husbands, parents or siblings because of what they reveal about 'family secrets'.

♦ One Tamil writer told us that her ex-husband broke her right wrist for daring to write a poem about their divorce; and many others spoke about the physical abuse they suffered in the marital home because of their writing.

♦ But the market and literary establishments have their own subtle and unremarked forms of censorship, and equally subtle manipulations that sometimes barely conceal outright bias.

♦ And that censorship emanates from many sources, and is chameleon-like: what was proscribed yesterday may be prescribed today but, equally, what is permitted today may be silenced tomorrow.

Ritu Menon on censoring Indian women writers 2002

♦ Many governments deny that their information controls amount to censorship: the British government denies that the ban on broadcasting statements by Sinn Fein and other Irish organisations amounts to censorship; the Allied forces in the Gulf War insisted that information was controlled for reasons of operational security.

♦ Censorship is a contested category. One person's censorship is another person's national security or religious custom.

♦ In western Europe, the most invidious form of censorship is self-censorship. Its minor evil is in hoodwinking readers into believing they have shared the author's full story; its greater evil in perpetuating the pleasant myth that we live in societies where free expression and open discourse are untrammelled.

♦ The London reader, unlike the reader in Pakistan, is falsely reassured that there is no censor snipping out sections of copy.

Gregory Palast 1999

DO WE NEED CENSORSHIP?
Michael Grade

Is censorship ever justified? The obvious knee-jerk response must of course be an emphatic no. Just as commercial markets can't function effectively and efficiently without freely available information between buyers and sellers, so democracy cannot flourish without a free flow of facts, ideas, opinions, and beliefs. Citizens can only make up their minds on any issue, large or small, if they live in an environment of unrestricted information, offering the widest range of potential input.

At the top for any society, politicians can only be called to account, and tyrannies prevented, if serious failures and improper uses of power can be made known to all citizens. That is the core justification of a free press, for all its manifest imperfections. That is precisely why dictators, oligarchs, juntas, emperors and tyrants through the ages have sought to censor debate and to stifle the free dissemination of opinion and information. Selective secrecy, as much as widespread fear, is the key tool of tyranny and dictatorship.

If it were as simple as that, there would of course be no debate. Who but an enemy of freedom and democracy would stand up for censorship if that were an end of it? We could all sign up to it, and smugly walk away.

The real world is more difficult. There are two perplexing areas where censorship is routinely advocated and defended by those who claim to be the friends of democracy: they are security and the protection of public morals. These are the two exceptions to the free flow of information and opinion that muddy the pursuit of absolute rights and freedoms, and that make the fight against censorship more an endless series of skirmishes than a single glorious war to be won.

The health of our democracies owes as much to past victories in the name of freedom of thought and expression as it does to the defeat of armies. In later mediaeval societies – especially after the invention of the printing press – censorship was the blunt instrument used by temporal and spiritual powers alike to enforce and extend control. It was a necessary – and often more potent – instrument than physical force. Now, the tide of democracy, accompanied by its philosophical and material emphasis on the rights of the individual, has rolled back the defence of censorship to those two issues of national security and public morality.

Of the two, the security issue – though complex – is easier to address. Clearly it would be absurd to allow real and potential enemies to threaten our society, by reckless publication, say, of information that would endanger national defence. After 9/11, the probability of further terrorist attacks must be a powerful argument for restricting information that would assist such attacks, by identifying targets, or revealing plans to combat them. I hope that self-restraint and common sense in the media will be the first line of defence here. Beyond that, if we agree that governments must proscribe any category of information, it should only happen under proper democratic scrutiny by our elected representatives. And that scrutiny must not be perfunctory, or offer blanket excuses for a creeping culture of secrecy. It must be specific, and it must be continuous.

We know all too well how governments of quite different stripes find it difficult to resist opportunities to conduct business away from the glare of public and media attention. When we agree – reluctantly and through the proper democratic process – that some censorship is necessary in the national interest, then we must remain vigilant that these exceptions do not expand beyond absolute necessity, and that they are ended as soon as possible. Censorship loves nothing better than mission creep in the stifling of ideas and information.

The question of public morals is more difficult. How legitimate are they? If so, how are they to be circumscribed, and not encroach on areas where they are, in ascending order of danger, unnecessary, inappropriate and a threat to freedom?

The other matter, the protection of public morals, also creates blurred edges to any absolute defence against censorship. Pornography may be the cause of actual physical harm, in its making or by those who would mimic it. We all share a particular horror of harm done to children. But even more than is the case with national security, we must constantly be on our guard to ensure that whatever safeguards we erect for these specific purposes are not hijacked by those who would be the moral police of innocent activities innocently pursued. The Roman Republic invented the censor, who regulated public morals as well as conducting the census from which he got his name. The Romans saw the inherent danger of the office, and posed the very pertinent question: *Quis custodiet ipsos custodes*? (Who guards the custodians?)

Many battles have been fought in the past against minorities who have sought to impose their own narrow standards of taste and decency on the rest of society. We have specific laws concerning defamation, blasphemy and obscene publications. We have film certification boards. We have regulators opining on the tastefulness or otherwise of radio and television programmes. They should all be subject to permanent scrutiny. Above all they should all be required to fit the mores of contemporary society, and not used to apply the supposed standards of an earlier age, no matter how vociferously small lobbying groups demand it.

In the age of the internet and 24-hour news services, we see and hear things from which were protected even 20 years ago. Some of it is disturbing. Some of it perhaps does do harm, and justifies calls for state intervention. But most of it has added to the richness of our information environment. It makes us wiser, better citizens, and is an asset to be cherished.

In a mature democracy there will always be debate about the role of censorship. It is unavoidable. But let it be restricted to issues of real and substantial harm, let it be subject to close and constant scrutiny and let it be ended promptly when its particular purpose has passed.

CHILDREN

♦ Vitya could have known worse. He might have been picked up for slave labour in Azerbaijan where, *Argumenty I Fakty* reports, children are kept as unpaid house servants by well-heeled families with an image to think about. He might have slipped into drug smuggling or prostitution, or ended up fruit-picking in an isolated settlement in the central Asian outback where children are said to work for 14–16 hours a day under armed guard. Or he might have been sold to the West, either for adoption or, as lurid Moscow tabloids claim, as an organ donor.

♦ Children now fend for themselves in the cellars and shattered apartment blocks of Grozny. They dart about in oversize ladies' sweaters and newly acquired green velvet berets begging, pilfering and sniffing glue. During the war they had the job of cycling round the city to check out the numbers of Russian Federal troops, their position and ammunition stores.

♦ But the hundreds of thousands of kids roaming Russian cities diving past you into the Moscow metro, whooping gleefully as they release yet another dog some hapless owner has left tied to a tree are, more often than not, merely preferring the questionable allure of the streets to abuse, violence and dipsomania at home.

♦ They shelter mostly in the attics of tenement blocks and in cellars, at railway stations and airports, in small groups with a teenage leader who acts as financial manager, housing adviser, judge and agent of punishment.

♦ It is a chilling sign of the times. But then eight out of 10 families in Russia live below the poverty line. Education, career prospects and entertainment are reserved for the privileged few.

Irena Maryniak 1997

♦ In 1979, 1 in 10 children in the UK lived below the poverty line; in 1996, it was 1 in 3, in 2002 it is still around that mark, with some calculations putting the figure closer to 1 in 2 in inner London

♦ In Liberia, children make up a quarter of all civil war combatants

♦ In the UK, children begin to worry about being too fat by the age of 8

♦ 1 million children work in the Asian sex trade

♦ 50% of Cambodians are under 15

♦ Ireland has the world's lowest infant mortality rate

♦ 2 million girls between 4 and 12 undergo genital mutilation every year

♦ There are 1,000–2,000 million child labourers worldwide

♦ The average age of the homeless in the USA is 9

Compiled by Jesse Banfield & Nevine Mabro 1997

♦ Over the last decade, some two million children have been killed in wars, six million seriously injured or disabled, and almost 30 million turned into refugees.

♦ As with the Convention on Torture, it is all something of a sham. The Convention on Children is being violated, systematically and contemptuously, and no countries violate it more energetically than those that were quickest to sign. Almost every ill it set out to remedy has grown worse in the years since it was drafted.

Caroline Moorehead 1997

♦ A century that began with children having virtually no rights is ending with them having the most powerful legal instrument that not only recognises but protects their human rights.

Carol Bellamy on the UN Convention on the Rights of the Child 1997

♦ Yet while politicians are quick to cite their devotion to children as an excuse for limiting the civil liberties of young and old alike, they are far less quick to adopt constructive measures that will actually advance young people's current wellbeing or future prospects.

Nadine Strossen 1995

♦ The machine harasses the youth; it jails, it tortures, it kills. They are the living proof of its importance.

It throws them out: it sells them as human flesh, cheap labour for foreign countries.

♦ The sterile machine hates everything that grows and moves. It's able only to multiply prisons and cemeteries. It can only produce prisoners and corpses, spies and policemen, beggars and exiles.

♦ Being young is a crime. Reality commits it every day at dawn; so does history, re-born every morning.

That is why reality and history are prohibited.

Eduardo Galeano 1978

♦ The 10-year-old girl soldier cocked her rifle, pointed it at his chest, and said she would shoot him if he didn't obey. And he obeyed her.

Adewale Maja-Pearce 1995

CORRUPTION

♦ By 1995, corruption [in China] had developed from the individual to an organisational stage, with leaders of social organisations utilising public authority entrusted to their institution or state apparatus for 'power-money exchanges'. Lower-level social organisations mobilised the public resources under their control to bribe upper-level organisations for more financial support, better administrative deals or business opportunities. In the Zhanjiang city corruption scandal, the party secretary, the mayor and leading government departments figures were involved – and caught. Similar exposures bedevil the army.

♦ Corruption developed to a systemic stage and has permeated the bulk of the party and state apparatus, becoming an established arrangement within institutions, as official posts are traded as counters in the redistribution of political, economic and cultural power. Official campaigns against corruption are no longer real threats to it but are instruments of political leverage and blackmail for personal gain. The power and wealth of the few keep them on top but the crudity of their route to enrichment means that society has no moral respect for them.

♦ Many corruption cases never reach the public eye. Judged by their behaviour, these are power-holders of very low quality.

He Qinglian 2002

♦ The European Court reported: 'There are recognised cases, for instance tourism, where files were withheld from UCLAF investigators (the anti-corruption agency that reports only to the Commission) and incriminating documents were systematically destroyed.'

♦ MEP Rosemarie Wernhauer, a German corruption expert, criticised the EU for protecting officials and for paying lawyers representing officials under investigation to hound journalists critical of its goings on. She found it 'legally reprehensible that the EU should decide for itself whether the law should apply to its own officials'.

♦ A libel action is being brought by Commission officials against the German magazine *Focus* for reporting a financial scandal, alleged by internal auditors, in the EC. The plaintiffs are demanding the equivalent of US$1 million in damages. Their legal costs are being funded with EU taxpayers' money by the Commission.

Anon 1998

DEATH

DEMOCRACY

DIASPORAS

DICTATORSHIP

DISAPPEARED

DISSENT

DRUGS

DEATH

♦ **Imagine**

Imagine living, eating, sleeping, relieving oneself, daydreaming, weeping – but mostly waiting – in a room about the size of your bathroom.

Now imagine doing all those things – but mostly waiting – for the rest of your life.

Imagine – waiting – waiting – to die.

I don't have to imagine.

I 'live' in one of those rooms, like about 3,000 other men and women in 37 states across the United States.

It's called 'Death Row'.

I call it 'Hell'.

Welcome to Hell.

A white, rural hell, where most of the caged captives are black and urban.

It is an American way of death.

Today the lowest-level politico up to the president use another sure-fire gimmick to guarantee victory.

Death.

Promise death and the election is yours.

Guaranteed.

Vraiment.

A 'Vote for Hell' in the 'Land of Liberty', with its over one million prisoners, is the ticket to victory.

Mumia Abu-Jamal 1995

♦ A recent note in the *New York Times* read 'Eleven days after he took office, George Pataki, New York's pro-death penalty governor, sent Thomas Grasso, a pro-death penalty murderer, back to Oklahoma to await death by lethal injection.' In America, capital punishment is so popular that even the denizens of death row support it! Populism rules and what populism wants, populism gets. A defendant on death row who has exculpatory evidence can now still be put to death if he fails to present that evidence past a certain deadline. But as it spreads across the states, the death penalty's installation is certain to prove a disappointment. Innocent people will infallibly be shot, given lethal injections. Like Mr Pataki's cynical prisoner, Mr Grasso, populists may learn to beware of what they demand, because they may just get it.

Christopher Hitchens 1995

♦ In 1980, the year Sierra Leone held the OAU conference, President Siaka Probyn Stevens built luxury villas for the delegates and flew in a fleet of limousines. Zebra crossings were hurriedly painted across streets and traffic lights put up all over the city with no regard whatever to road planning. The PZ department store was filled with luxury imported goods, and yet the country was in hock, hopelessly in debt for generations to come – the money used to finance Stevens' power. When the head of the national bank denounced this vast expenditure, Stevens had the man dragged from his bed at night and thrown out the window.

♦ The 1996 elections were hailed as a triumph of civil society. But democracy was as effective as a sticking plaster on a gaping head wound. By then all formal structures of government had eroded or been dismantled.

Aminatta Forna 2002

♦ A debate about the right to die would have seemed off to people in imperial Rome. If a slave held a sword for his master to run into or fall on, or if a servant or family member helped mix poison into wine for someone ready to depart, there was no question of either the principal or the assistant in the case being held blameable, either morally or in law.

♦ Christian ethics brought about a complete change in the acceptability of such practices. The idea that life is sacred because 'God-given' introduced a proscription on the taking of life that has been construed in blanket terms when viewed from the perspective of practices such as abortion, infanticide and euthanasia.

♦ The problem of the 'right to die' arises directly from the conflict of intuitions between the lingering Judaeo-Christian view and the secular morality underlying human rights thinking since the eighteenth-century Enlightenment.

AC Grayling 2002

♦ To please no one will I prescribe a deadly drug, or give advice which may cause my patient's death.

The Hippocratic Oath

DEMOCRACY

♦ The classic definition of democracy is not majority rule, but the protection of minorities.

Darryl Pinckney 1996

♦ Democracy can only work in an atmosphere of respect for, and promotion of, collective human rights. Human rights, in turn, presuppose an understanding of humans as an end in themselves and never a means to an end.

Leonardo Boff 1999

♦ Conformism is dangerous. It's the foundation of totalitarianism. A society predisposed to conformism will succumb.

Vladimir Bukovsky 2001

♦ Post-war European democracy has always depended for its existence on a successful consumer capitalism.

Nicholas Fraser 2001

♦ 'People are being choked by democracy and freedom,' a Jesuit priest told me.

Irena Maryniak on Poland 1994

♦ An intellectual is there to form the critical conscience of a democracy: that's what I'm trying to do.

Adam Michnik on Poland 1994

♦ The abstract term 'equality' took on materiality as we moved towards the church hall polling station and the simple act, the drawing of an X, that ended over three centuries of privilege for some, deprivation of human dignity for others.

Nadine Gordimer on South Africa 1994

♦ Perhaps the most impressive development is the growth of loud calls to extend democracy to global institutions as different as the World Trade Organisation, the International Olympic Committee and the United Nations. Talk of 'global democracy' is unprecedented and, not surprisingly, in certain quarters eyebrows are rising at the suggestion that the methods and ideals of democracy can be stretched so far. There is talk of 'overstretch' and of how democracies have a history of self-destruction by the hubris of their own democratic methods.

♦ Plato's rule: affairs of government are too complex and difficult to explain to publics

John Keane 2002

♦ Controlling military power is democracy's enduring challenge; secret military and intelligence power is the most difficult to control. The press has begun to uncover special operations mistakes in Afghanistan and it must do more, or we will have no control whatever over the war waged in our name.

Michael Ignatieff 2002

♦ The tragedy that began with the military dictatorship in March 1976, the most terrible our nation has ever suffered, will undoubtedly serve to help us understand that it is only democracy that can save a people from a horror on this scale.

Ernesto Sábato on Argentina 1986

DIASPORAS

♦ Commodified exoticism – ethnic otherness in cuisine, fashion, music, film and literature – effectively silences less easily consumable voices.

Tom Cheesman and Marie Gillespie 2002

♦ The problem with the predominance of cosmopolitan diasporic writing is in the absence of that other diasporic voice, in the silencing of the men and women who arrive in Europe not safely buckled into their seats, but clinging frozen to the undercarriage of aeroplanes and trains, or suffocated in the backs of lorries and vans.

Akash Kapur 2002

♦ Little India in Manhattan is where the diaspora meets to indulge in nostalgia.

Salil Tripathi 2002

♦ Our grandchildren understand more about British culture, British festivals than they understand about ours. We wish they did know more. But since they live here in England, we cannot compel them. They don't know any Chinese characters. They can't read Chinese. But then I can't read Chinese either.

Mrs Cheng 2000

DICTATORSHIP

♦ The list of torturings, murders and disappearances does not exhaust the crimes of a dictatorship. The machine trains you to egoism and lies. Solidarity is a crime. Victory for the machine: people are afraid of speaking, of looking at each other.

♦ No one is to meet anyone else. When someone meets your eyes and doesn't look away you think: 'He's going to get me.' The manager says to the employee who was his friend: 'I had to report you. They asked for lists. I had to give a name. Forgive me, if you can.'

♦ Why doesn't murder of the soul by poisoning figure in the chronicle of violence?

Eduardo Galeano on Uruguay 1978

♦ The failure of the long-overdue parliamentary elections [in Belarus] in May 1995 (there was insufficient turnout in 141 constituencies) allowed him [Alyaksandr Lukashenka] six months of rule by decree. The country was peppered with directives which included a list of cadres not allowed to leave the country without his written consent (among others, university administrators and the editors of major newspapers) and a blanket ban on all textbooks in the humanities published since 1992. Many of his fiats have been ruled illegal by the Constitutional Court;

but Lukashenka does not recognise its competence. He operates by a simple syllogism: the constitution says Belarus is a presidential republic, he is the president, therefore any decision he takes is constitutional and anyone who opposes him is in breach of the constitution.

Vera Rich on Belarus 1996

♦ One does not enlist in the Resistance – in that mortally dangerous confrontation with the all-powerful persecution mechanism of a dictatorship, where the chances of being caught are far greater than the chances of getting away with it, where arrest will result in the most unbearable and long-term suffering – one doesn't get involved in all this without some very strong personal motive.

♦ From the moment my country was humiliated, debased, it was inevitable that I should go underground.

George Mangakis on Greece 1972

♦ The question that is often asked of us is how the dictatorship affects one's personal life. Has it really made all that difference? Is there real hardship, and real oppression? In the first year of the dictatorship, quite a lot of people answered that question with: 'As long as you mind your own business, you can live quite happily and peacefully.' Apart from the fact that quite a large number of people are not *able* to reduce their lives to 'minding their own business', it seems to me that not even this contention is true. Most people have found that sooner or later, no matter what their position is, some demand will be made, some sign of submission or conformity will be required of them.

Anonymous Greek writer 1972

♦ Police archives are the legacy of all dictatorships. They are a time bomb. When they explode, they destroy.

Adam Michnik 1996

♦ Democracy is uncertainty, risk and responsibility, but it seldom enforces its policies through violence. Dictatorship means violence daily; it is fear,

humiliation and silence. But it is the charm of dictatorship that it
liberates people from responsibility: the state answers for everything.
You cease to become a citizen and become state property.

Adam Michnik 1998

DISAPPEARED

♦ This civil aviation pilot's life abruptly changed direction the day he
found the corpses of two of his children in a common grave, a few weeks
after they 'vanished' at the end of January 1995. Since then, Khamidov,
elegantly dressed in grey suit and tie, has devoted himself entirely to
the task of uncovering the slaughter-houses and ossuaries scattered
throughout Chechen territory and to photographing the victims.

♦ As we talk, a man appears who has 11 disappeared in his family: he
comes daily, hopeful new 'finds' will allow him to bury one of them.

Juan Goytisolo 1996

♦ In October 1999, an organisation called the Committee of the Families
of the Kidnapped and Disappeared in Lebanon sought to remind the
government of the 17,000 or so people who vanished between 1975 and
1990, the long night of Lebanon's wars. The committee, established in
West Beirut in 1982, launched a campaign to find common ground with
the authorities, who have assiduously avoided investigating the fate of
the disappeared.

♦ Many of those abducted vanished without a trace; where, they ask,
does one hide 17,000 corpses?

Michael Young 2000

♦ In legal terms, a pardon implies not the abolition of guilt but a relief
from punishment. On the other hand, an amnesty (such as the military
had granted itself *in extremis* in 1982 and which was repealed by
Alfonsin) is, in effect, a recognition of innocence that wipes away
any imputation of crime.

♦ No deed, however monstrous or trivial, can ever be abolished once committed.

♦ The pardon granted by a victim – the dripping quality of mercy – has no bearing on the mechanics of justice.

♦ Menem's amnesty, bowing to the demands of acknowledged murderers and torturers, has postponed the healing for what appears to be a very long time.

Alberto Manguel on Argentina's Disappeared 1996

♦ Thus, in the name of national security, thousands upon thousands of human beings, usually young adults or even adolescents, fell into the sinister, ghostly category of the *desaparecidos,* a word (sad privilege for Argentina) frequently left in Spanish by the world's press.

♦ A feeling of complete vulnerability spread throughout Argentine society, coupled with the fear that anyone, however innocent, might become a victim of the never-ending witch-hunt.

♦ From the moment of their abduction, the victims lost all rights. Deprived of all communication with the outside world, held in unknown places, subjected to barbaric tortures, kept ignorant of their immediate or ultimate fate, they risked being either thrown into the river or sea, weighed down with blocks of cement, or burned to ashes.

Ernesto Sábato 1986

DISSENT

♦ So where do we go for freedom, and who can we rely on to voice that dissent without which a society stagnates, however well the economy may be doing? We are left with writers and journalists no doubt, and the Church unexpectedly enough. No doubt journalists have a heavy responsibility to be forever watchful, and many discharge it admirably. But the times are not propitious. In healthier days most newspapers, certainly those which were the most readable, attacked the government

of the day, whichever government it might be. Now, however, too many journalists censor themselves, and the temptation to write what they fear the proprietor or the editor may require is no doubt hard to resist . . . Sadly, young writers who should be manning the barricades against such monstrosities as the new Secrets reform are merely muttering approval, like clubland bores. Perhaps they will read all this and say, well, we're better off than the Russians or the South Africans so what on earth is the point of complaining? In answer to this I can only go back, as I so often do, to Wordsworth.

> We must be free or die, who speak the tongue
> That Shakespeare spake; the faith and morals hold
> Which Milton held . . .

But then Wordsworth, of course, was born before Mrs Whitehouse said her prayers.

John Mortimer 1988

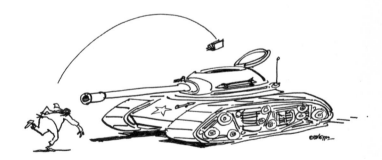

♦ Only a few people dare to confront their political environment, their neighbours, their families by signalling disbelief or even dissent with government opinion.

Dusan Reljic on Serbia 1999

♦ Football dissidence can be defined as follows: expressing dissent against a regime by supporting football teams that play against the regime's team. Often, in a dictatorship, football dissidence is the only available form of mass dissent. So strong was football dissidence in eastern Europe that for many people it seems to have been the main motive for watching matches. It is noteworthy that in Albania, the most repressive state in Communist Europe, football attendance per head of population was the highest in Europe in the 1980s.

Simon Kuper 2000

♦ Where is America now? Ask another American and you'd get another answer, but here's mine: America is at a place where I cannot burn the nation's flag and call it legal protest, but the Ku Klux Klan can burn a cross in a public place and call it religion.

Josh Passell 1995

♦ We became dissidents without actually knowing how, and we found ourselves behind bars without really knowing how. We simply did certain things we had to do and that seemed proper to do: nothing more nor less.

Václav Havel 1979

WAR ON DRUGS
Howard Marks

Recreational drugs (substances consumed for purposes other than medical treatment or sustenance) can change one's feelings, thoughts, perceptions and behaviour: they can change one's state of mind.

One's state of mind may be changed physically (hang-gliding or fasting), spiritually (talking to witch doctors or undergoing purification rituals) or psychologically (being hypnotised or psychoanalysed). Generally, the activity of changing states of minds is permitted, if not approved and encouraged, by the powers that be. One hundred years ago, any respectable person could walk into a chemist in Britain and choose from a range of cannabis tinctures, hashish pastes, cocaine lozenges and opium extracts. He could immediately purchase morphine, heroin and a hypodermic syringe and could place an order for mescaline. But for the past 80 years, authority has not so approved. Even though most people take recreational drugs (as they always have) the possession and trade of most recreational drugs (excepting, in some countries, alcohol and tobacco) have relatively recently been criminalised under a strategy of prohibition often referred to as the 'War on Drugs'.

According to Rousseau's social contract, society emerges from an agreement between the citizens and an elected sub-group, the state. In exchange for upholding their liberties by the rule of law, the citizens agree to empower the state by paying taxes. Insufficient law yields anarchy (American firearms laws). Excessive law yields tyranny (Iranian religious law). Western jurisdictions have sought the optimum by forbidding acts harmful to others but allowing those that are not, including any that are harmful only to oneself. First applied officially by von Humboldt in 1810, it is known as 'consenting adults in private' legislation. Prostitution, homosexuality and even suicide are no longer crimes. The only exception is the taking of recreational drugs, prevented by the very costly 'War on Drugs'.

We are asked to consider whether the 'War on Drugs' (a phrase coined by United States President Richard Nixon when he formed the United States Drug Enforcement Administration in 1972) provides a protection necessary for society's well-being. Does it clearly reduce any harm caused by people's desire to take recreational drugs or is it simply a means of social control, be it benign (preventing the spread of disease, unemployment, dysfunctional and criminal behaviour) or more sinister (ensuring that ignorant and meddlesome outsiders such as ourselves don't interfere with the work of the serious people who run public affairs)?

I find it impossible to accept the view that protection against the taking of one's own life is less necessary than protection against the consumption of recreational drugs. If the so-called necessary protection mandated is merely mis-guided or overvalued, then authority could be forgiven for its imposition. But since the War on Drugs was implemented, drug use has risen at an unprecedented pace. Two-thirds of all registered voters under the age of 25 take soft drugs and have access to harder drugs if they want them. Everyone who wants to take drugs is already taking drugs. This clearly means the War on Drugs is not working, even from the prohibitionist's point of view.

Apart from not achieving its aims, the War on Drugs also makes drugs artificially expensive and spawns an avalanche of acquisitive criminal behaviour. The illegal drug business has become so profitable that there are violent fights over territory in which to sell drugs. Across the Middle East, South-East Asia, Africa and Latin America, civil war after civil war has been funded by the only strategy available to revolutionaries and counter-revolutionaries alike – the mass production of their traditional drugs for sale to the absurdly lucrative global market.

The War on Drugs drives out socially controlled, relatively safe drugs such as opium and coca, and promotes the consumption of adulterated concentrates such as heroin and cocaine. There are no controls in a black market, so some illegal drugs might be mixed with dangerous substances. People dilute and adulterate illegal drugs to make more money. Black-market drugs are of variable strength, and can cause accidental and fatal overdoses. Black-market drugs are often administered dangerously because of inadequate education and resources, resulting in serious infections such as Aids or hepatitis B.

Some recreational drugs can definitely have adverse effects on health. The War on Drugs makes them more dangerous, and fails to reduce their use. The War on Drugs increases any harm that might be caused by recreational drug use. A recreational drug cannot by virtue of its chemical nature cause crime; it can only do so within a social context, which is the War on Drugs and the consequent black market. The War on Drugs is therefore a root cause of crime, violence and ill health.

The War on Drugs is not about benign social control but instead the abrogation of such social control, leading to unregulated peddling of adulterated substances outside the reach of the law. It would be difficult to construct a policy more physically dangerous, more individually criminalising or more socially destructive. Accordingly, any social control accompanying the War on Drugs is probably motivated by the desire to keep the populace passive, apathetic and obedient and prevent them from interfering with privilege and power. One of the traditional and obvious ways of controlling people in society, whether it's a military dictatorship or a democracy, is to frighten them so that they'll accord authority to their superiors who claim they will protect them. The War on Drugs creates fear of people from whom we have to protect ourselves. It also takes care of superfluous people who don't contribute to profit making and wealth (in the US, this tends to mean the poor and black): they're put in prison. The War on Drugs protects no one outside a small elite group, endangers everyone else and is a sinister means of social control.

E

EDUCATION
ENVIRONMENT
ETHICS
ETHNIC CLEANSING
EXILE

EDUCATION

♦ 'Education shall be directed to the full development of the human personality and to the strengthening of respect for human rights and fundamental freedoms.'

♦ 'Everyone has the right to education. Education shall be free, at least in the elementary and fundamental stages. Elementary education shall be compulsory.'

Universal Declaration of Human Rights Article 26

♦ The discourse around education as a human right sometimes overlooks an important factor: what it means to be human in any society differs for women and men.

Naila Kabeer 1998

♦ I have not studied, I can just write my name. In the village, they do not educate girls. But though I have no education, we must still educate our daughters.

Sufia Begum 1998

♦ I don't want my daughters to be like me, uneducated. When I went to get the loan, I could not sign my name. I was so ashamed in front of so many people. That is why I would like to educate them so that they need never feel ashamed.

Zahera Khatoon 1998

POLITICAL OPINIONS:
SHOULD THEY BE KEPT OUT OF TEACHING?
Chris Woodhead

'What do you think?' our children are asked, lesson after lesson, day after day. They are probably asked how they feel even more often, but it is a close-run thing. Everybody must empathise and introspect; everybody, however ignorant, must have an opinion. What matters these days is the critical engagement, the process of thought, the honing of judgement. And the relevance, of course, of what is discussed to the social, economic and political realities that lie beyond the classroom. Gone are the bad, old Gradgrindian days when the teacher, an authority in his or her subject, taught children things they did not know. 'We now know', Professor John MacBeath of Cambridge University writes, 'that "far from thinking coming after knowledge, knowledge comes on the coat tails of thinking". Instead of knowledge-based schools we need thinking-centred schools.'

So, yes, why not? Let us bring political opinions right into the heart of the classroom. We shall need, of course, to ensure that children are not exposed to blatant propaganda, but that is not difficult. The teacher simply becomes a 'neutral chairman' who holds the ring. Nothing could be easier. The fact that they do not know enough to have an opinion is neither here nor there. 'Knowledge comes on the coat tails of thinking', stupid. Let our children engage with the great political questions of the day and they will come, naturally and inevitably, to assimilate whatever knowledge and understanding they need. Like most of the orthodoxies peddled so enthusiastically by the great and the good of the education establishment, it sounds wonderful, doesn't it?

In fact, it is a recipe for yet further disaster. Here is someone who understands rather more about teaching than the Cambridge professor I have just quoted: Jonathan Smith, who taught English for 30 years at Tonbridge. 'The best teachers', he observes, 'tell you things. Now the pupil is told less, and yet, paradoxically, the less he is told the more he is being told to think for himself.' Primary school teachers are expected to give their seven-year-olds the opportunity 'to find out about the main political and social institutions that affect their lives'. Children, for their part, must learn 'to understand and respect our common humanity, diversity and differences so that they can go on to form effective, fulfilling relationships that are an essential part of life and learning'.

What bothers me most is not the possibility of indoctrination, though this is real and serious. It is, rather, the sheer Alice in Wonderland unreality of those who want to substitute these cosmic aspirations for the teaching of basic skills and knowledge. For, obviously enough, the more time that is devoted, in primary or secondary classrooms, to the exploration of political opinion, the less time there is for the mastery of that learning upon which any serious exploration of the issues that affect our 'common humanity' depends. Why, the National Curriculum Order for Citizenship asks, is world peace so elusive? Why indeed? In my mid-50s, I am hard pushed to marshal a half-coherent response. But this is a question the government believes primary school children can ponder in a meaningful way. It is ridiculous, and a ridiculous waste of time that ought to be used for genuinely educational purposes. Is it surprising that 200,000 seven-year-olds cannot read?

When George Walden was MP for Buckingham he paid a visit to one of his local primary schools. He stood watching a history lesson. The subject was the French resistance. The children clearly had very little idea who was resisting what, or even where France might be. But this did not matter. The teacher was telling the class how a little girl had had to watch her father being dragged off by the Gestapo. 'How', the teacher asked (yes, you have guessed it), 'would you have felt if you had been that little girl and it was your father?' Silence, George noted, reigned. Then one pupil, eyes screwed up in concentration, deliberated and delivered the expected reply: 'I would not have liked it, Miss.'

This is the banal endgame, the inevitable consequence of a hostility to the teaching of real knowledge on the one hand, and a determination on the other to push the pupil's emotional and intellectual response centre stage. The truth is that we need less politics in the classroom, less opinion generally. Forget the rhetoric of citizenship and the strident calls to render the curriculum more student-centred, more politically relevant. The truth today is that 27% of respondents to a recent poll did not realise that joining the euro means scrapping the pound. Only half of a random survey of 18-year-olds knew that the Battle of Britain took place in

1940. Seven per cent thought that it took place in 1066 and that the troops involved were cavalry.

We can encourage our children to spout ill-informed prejudice. We can applaud their attempts to criticise and question accepted opinion. We can, unrealistically, expect the teachers who have to conduct such lessons to maintain a studied, impenetrable neutrality. Or we can revert to a traditional belief in education as a transaction between the generations in which what matters is not the sound and fury of the immediate political controversy but the best that has been thought and known. Sadly, I do not think that any of us should hold our breath.

A. KRAUZE

ENVIRONMENT

♦ As issues concerning the health of the planet appear to creep up the news agenda – partly, say analysts, in response to a perceived ecological crisis and partly because of events such as the Earth Summit in Johannesburg – press freedom organisations have warned of the increasing dangers facing journalists reporting on environmental affairs. Igor Kravchuk, a reporter with the Russian daily *Vesti*, revealed that impoverished sailors from Russia's northern pacific port were stripping submarines of communications equipment and radioactive components to sell to organised crime. While covering the trial of two sailors accused of selling equipment, he was threatened with jail.

Andrew Wasley 2003

♦ Reporting on the environment in the Philippines is about power. A handful of families control the country's forests, coastal resources and land; and they are wealthy, well connected and entrenched. That is why environmental reporting is not safe.

Marites Vitug 2003

♦ Corporate ownership of the media has affected the nature of coverage of environmental issues.

Aidan White 2003

ETHICS

♦ Duties of the journalist:

1. To respect truth, whatever be the consequences to himself.

2. To defend freedom of information, comment and criticism.

3. To report only on facts of which he knows the origin; not to suppress essential information or alter texts and documents.

4. Not to use unfair methods to obtain news, photographs or documents.

5. To restrict himself to the respect of privacy.

6. To rectify any published information which is found to be inaccurate.

7. To observe professional secrecy and not to divulge the source of information obtained in confidence.

8. To regard as grave professional offences plagiarism, calumny, slander, libel and unfounded accusations, the acceptance of bribes in any form in consideration of either publication or suppression of news.

9. Never to confuse the profession of journalist with that of advertisements salesman or propagandist and to refuse any direct or indirect orders from advertisers.

10. To resist every pressure and to accept editorial orders only from the responsible persons of the editorial staff.

Declaration of the rights and obligations of journalists (The Munich Charter) 1971

ETHNIC CLEANSING

♦ From Bosnia to Rwanda the forcible expulsion of rival ethnic groups has become the measure of the breakdown of civilised values.

Kenan Malik 1997

♦ Ogoniland is the first Nigerian experimentation with 'ethnic cleansing', authorised and sustained by the Nigerian despot, General Sani Abacha. His on-the-spot operatives, Lt-Colonel Dauda Komo and Major Paul Okutimo, are Nigeria's contribution to the world's shameful directory of obedience to orders over and above the call of duty. The so-called 'Task Force on Internal Security' is doomed to be Abacha's sole legacy to the nation, Nigeria's yet unheralded membership card of the club of the practitioners of 'ethnic cleansing' . . .

Wole Soyinka 1994

♦ So while it would have been easier if the goblins could have made the Muslims or the Serbs and their houses simply disappear, one does the best one can with dynamite and bulldozers. Obliterating the memory of a place – making lives and communities as though they had never been – must be one of the ultimate forms of censorship.

♦ There is an actual map which explains better than any narrative the complexity out of which all this came. This ethnographic map of Bosnia from the 1991 census must be one of the most extraordinary exhibits in the history of cartography, just as Bosnia's melting-pot was one of Europe's most curious pieces of nation-making. It shows at a glance the dense and complicated distribution of the Serb, Croat and Muslim mix across all the country's corrugation of mountains and valleys. Compare it with the maps of the ceasefire and what is known of the Dayton maps, and you see almost as quickly how few people are now at home in Bosnia. First, the Muslims of the eastern towns and villages above the Brina, whose centuries-old culture is recreated in the novels of Ivo Andric, were driven west. Then, late in the war, the Krjina (border) Serbs, descendants of those planted by the Hapsburgs three centuries ago, to stiffen the Croatian frontier against the Turk, were herded east by the US-backed Croat and Bosnian offensives of last May and August in the war's biggest ethnic cleansing – 200,000 or more driven into bulging Banja Luka and its hinterland – or replanted in unwelcoming Kosovo.

♦ In Tuzla, that other celebrated example of the tradition Izetbegovic invoked, the ethnographic balance has been even more radically disturbed. Before the war, the 1991 census gave the proportion of Muslims to Serbs and Croats as roughly three to one; by 1995, UNHCR estimates showed, the tides of war had altered that proportion to 20 to one. The departure of many Serbs and Croats (though we saw some still in the surrounding villages, their churches undamaged), and the immense influx of Muslim refugees, leaving no billets for the hapless US troops whose headquarters the town has become, had made Tuzla statistically into a Muslim stronghold. In northern and eastern Bosnia-Herzegovina, the position is brutally reversed, the Muslim populations being reduced from 355,956 to 30,000 and 261,000 to 4,000 respectively.

WL Webb on former Yugoslavia 1996

EXILE

♦ The theme of exile appears to hold great fascination for literary critics, mere artistic consumers, anthologists and festival directors of all artistic genres.

♦ Literary history and sociology are incomplete without colourful, intrigue-filled accounts of (national) colonies of exiles – a familiar enough categorisation for those literary and artistic émigrés who swamped the congenial cafés of Paris both during the Tsarist era and following the Bolshevik Revolution.

♦ If there was ever an image that is appropriate and definitive on the liminal but dynamic condition of the exiled writer, the parachutist or free-fall glider is surely a front-runner.

♦ Over any state of mind we may arm ourselves with the challenging power of the will and thus negate all debilitating tendencies that threaten the ego from the inescapable fact of exile. Still, the questions persist, prodded into being by a sensation of loss, absence – however temporary – and by whatever strategies are adopted by individuals to counter the interruption in, or distortion of, their routine sense of being.

♦ Is there a moment when, on arriving there, one knows intuitively, and accepts that one has truly arrived in exile? (For now, we may postpone the complex but very real experience of exile as a state of mind that separates present consciousness from originating zone of self-cognisance: in short, exile as a home of alienation.)

♦ Exile may hanker for a sympathetic environment; one that trails an umbilical cord to abandoned roots, as if a handful of earth had been sneaked into the baggage and delivered ahead of the wanderer at his destination.

Wole Soyinka 2002

♦ Almost all foundations of philosophy and literature of the twentieth century – such as Marx, Freud, Joyce and Mann – were built on a sense of exile, and this has profoundly affected knowledge of the self and existence.

Yang Lian 2002

♦ Someone who is totally aware of themselves is always in exile. Once you peel away those layers that other people attach to you and reinforce, you gradually but firmly establish your own worth – and this includes self-doubt.

Gao Xingjian 2002

F

FATWA

FLM

FRST AMENDMENT

FREE EXPRESSION

FREEDOM

FREEDOM OF
INFORMATION

FATWA

♦ Rushdie is under a life-long threat of death issued by a sovereign state because he expressed views with which that state disagrees. Mr Rushdie, therefore, enjoys neither freedom of expression, freedom of movement, freedom of association, freedom of religion nor freedom from arbitrary assassination.

Judith Moses 1994

♦ **15 February 1989** The day after the *fatwa* on Salman Rushdie was announced:

Thousands of demonstrators chanting 'death to Britain' stone the British Embassy in Tehran (re-opened the previous November after an eight-year closure).

Iranian Foreign Minister Ali Akbar Velayati calls for an emergency meeting of the Islamic Conference Organisation to debate *The Satanic Verses* and calls upon all Muslim countries to close British and American cultural centres.

All Viking-Penguin books are banned from Iran.

Viking-Penguin's New York offices are evacuated for an hour after an anonymous bomb threat.

On television in Iran, Hojatoleslam Hassani Sanei, an Iranian cleric of the 15 Khordad Foundation, offers a US$3 million reward to any Iranian and £1 million to any foreigner who kills Salman Rushdie.

♦ **July 1993** Aziz Nesin, publisher of *The Satanic Verses* in Turkey, victim of an arson attack on his hotel which killed 37 people, though Nesin himself escaped.

♦ **October 1993** William Nygaard, Norwegian publisher of *The Satanic Verses*, shot three times.

'I inform the proud Muslim people of the world that the author of *The Satanic Verses* book which is against Islam, the Prophet and the Koran, and all involved in its publication who were aware of its content, are sentenced to death.' Any one who dies in the cause of ridding the world of Rushdie, said Ayatollah Ruhollah Khomeini of Iran, 'will be regarded as a martyr and go directly to heaven.'

Fiction, Fact and the Fatwa: A Chronology of Censorship

♦ I told them, these individuals are not guilty. The system is. I blame past and present Turkish governments for these incidents. Their policies have deliberately brought Islamic fundamentalism to this dangerous point.

♦ If the fundamentalists want to kill me, they will anyway. Why should another person die trying to protect me?

Aziz Nesin, Turkish translator of Salman Rushdie's *The Satanic Verses* 1994

♦ I don't have to run for my life any more. There is no *fatwa* or demonstrations against me. And no spontaneous flow of writing in my life any more. I want to write again. But for the last year I could write nothing but poems. . . . I could describe only my cravings to be a bird and fly back to my beloved Bangladesh.

♦ I too was caught in the wintry coldness of imprisonment in my country when the *fatwa* was announced against me, when they put a price on my head. It was Europe that gave me shelter and saved my life.

Taslima Nasrin 1996

♦ The Muslims thought it was immoral to bring 92 women to Nigeria [for the Miss World contest] and ask them to revel in vanity. What would [the Prophet] Mohammed think? In all honesty he would probably have chosen a wife from among them.

Isioma Daniel in *This Day* 18 November 2002 Nigeria

[As a result of the above, a fatwa calling for Ms Daniel's death was issued by Islamic authorities and the journalist fled to the USA. Ed]

FILM

♦ Since its early days the movie industry has been in an unholy (though some would say a holy) alliance with the censors. Censorship had shaped the course of movie history and played a part in determining the language of popular cinema. It would thus be as unrealistic and disingenuous to refuse the censor a seat at the centennial feast as it would have been, 40 years ago, to deny the public hangman an invitation to a celebration of British penology.

♦ Even before the first films were projected for a paying audience by the Lumière brothers in December 1895, the police had been intervening in Europe and North America to prevent peep-show machines from showing such innocently erotic items as *Dorolita's Passion Dance*, which was withdrawn in 1894 from the Kinetoscope Arcade on Atlantic City's Boardwalk.

♦ Shortly after the turn of the century, a Chicago judge claimed that the cinema was among the chief influences – bad, of course – on the juvenile offenders who appeared before him. His sentiments were echoed over 90 years later when the English judge in the James Bulger murder trial suggested that the juvenile killers had been influenced by the American horror movie *Child's Play 3*, though the local police could find no evidence that the children had seen it.

♦ Wherever films were made or shown, censorship boards sprang up. This led to the creation in 1912 of the British Board of Film Censors, initiated by the Home Office but run as a self-regulating body by the film industry, to license movies for public exhibition. Its second president, the ubiquitous TP O'Connor, Conservative MP, author and newspaper editor, served from 1916 until his death in 1929. During his reign, he made the film industry the acquiescent creature of the political establishment, a position from which it has yet to emerge.

♦ Alfred Hitchcock turned away from political film-making forever when his plans to make a picture about the 1926 General Strike were rejected by the BBFC.

♦ Will H Hays believed in the 'Ten Commandments, self-discipline, faith in time of trouble, worship, the Bible and the Golden Rule', and at one of his first Hollywood press conferences he declared: 'This industry must have towards the sacred thing, the mind of a child, towards that clean, virgin thing, that unmarked slate, the same responsibility, the same care about the impressions made upon it, that the best clergyman or the most inspired teacher would have.'

♦ This Hays Office Code, made mandatory in 1934, began with three general principles – 'no picture shall be produced that will lower moral standards'; 'correct standards of life, subject only to the requirements of drama and entertainment, shall be presented'; 'law, natural or human, shall not be ridiculed, nor shall sympathy be created for its violation.'

♦ When Hollywood bowed to the House Un-American Activities Committee (HUAC) and other McCarthyite witch-hunters in the post-World War II years, a group of blacklisted film-makers produced *Salt of the Earth* (1953), an independent film about a miners' strike in New Mexico. They were harassed while on location by local and federal authorities, the leading actress was deported to her native Mexico, and the completed film was denied exhibition in the USA until the 1960s when it became a cult work among student radicals.

♦ The European dictators of both left and right – Lenin and Stalin, Hitler and Mussolini – were fascinated by the cinema and aware of its power. They therefore sought to exploit it in their own interests.

♦ As the first great mass medium, the cinema provided the politicians and guardians of morality with the paradigm for censorship in the twentieth century.

♦ The simple fact is that at every societal level we have been inculcated with the idea that censorship is necessary – to preserve society, to protect people from each other, to save ourselves from our baser instincts. Revolution, personal violence and sex forever lurk to disturb the status quo. And censorship is most evident in the cinema because, unlike books, plays, exhibitions, TV programmes and the radio, every film we see, every video we buy, is prefaced on the screen or on the cassette box by a certificate stating that the work has been examined . . . and judged fit for us to see. It isn't in the interests of the film companies to reveal what the censor has excised for cinematic exhibition or video release.

♦ One might suppose that there was enough official supervision. Sadly, the press, both popular and elitist, tabloid and broadsheet, are among the first to demand tighter control of the movies, especially when it claims some gruesome murder has been influenced by a recent film.

♦ Looking back over a century of movie censorship, like Beaumarchais's *Figaro*, one laughs for fear that one might cry at the fatuity and foolishness of it all.

Philip French 1995

♦ Movies – which arouse special, private, hidden feelings – can overwhelm us as no other art form, except, perhaps, opera, does.

Pauline Kael 1995

♦ The final question about censorship and cinema is about what we ourselves are willing to look at – and how we construe what we see.

Edward Lucie-Smith 1998

♦ There is a growing body of evidence establishing the link between films and violent behaviour, particularly in the case of children watching without adult supervision

Anne Nelson 1994

♦ The biggest impetus to the will to censor is the idea that the media have 'effects' upon us.

Julian Petley 1994

♦ The accumulated evidence does not warrant the conclusion that viewing violent/pornographic films and videos is directly linked to violent criminal behaviour in the vast majority of cases.

"Video Violence and Young Offenders' (Association of Chief Police Officers) 1994

♦ If a film suggests an alternative view of a sensitive subject, it may be attacked before it is seen. Ireland is a case in point. Films that have attempted to tell Irish history from a neutral or Irish perspective are usually vilified in advance.

♦ So-called liberal and democratic societies have their own means of censorship, more insidious than the bureaucrat in his office.

Ken Loach 1995

♦ **5 June 1990** An announcement that an application will be made to issue in the UK, in video form, *International Guerillas*, a three-hour-long movie, which is breaking box office records in Pakistan. The film's plot is based upon the exploits of three Pakistani warriors who have sworn to seek out and kill Salman Rushdie, who is depicted as an anti-Islamic, drunken, sadistic murderer, hiding on a Pacific island protected by hundreds of Israeli soldiers.

♦ **22 July 1990** The British Board of Film classification refuses distribution rights to *International Guerillas* video, on grounds that the film is potentially libellous of Salman Rushdie.

Fiction, Fact and the Fatwa: A Chronology of Censorship

FIRST AMENDMENT

♦ 'Congress shall make no law respecting an establishment of religion, or prohibiting the free exercise thereof; or abridging the freedom of speech, or of the press; or the right of the people peaceably to assemble, and to petition the government for a redress of grievances.'

The First Amendment to the US Constitution 1789

♦ The First Amendment, Professor Henry Louis Gates Jr reminded his readers, is 'the very amendment that licensed the protests, the rallies, the organisation and the agitation', led by Dr Martin Luther King Jr and others, that so drastically changed the old racial order in the south.

Anthony Lewis 1995

♦ Shamelessly, the tobacco companies claim the limited protection afforded under the First Amendment to so-called 'commercial speech'.

♦ The ruling specifically recognised that 'child pornography and cigarette advertising' will never be fully protected by the First Amendment.

Peter Pringle 1996

FREE EXPRESSION

♦ A generation which takes freedom for granted has no inkling how to defend it.

♦ The generation for whom freedom is akin to nature, something outside the reaches of human will, has accepted its loss as something which cannot be resisted.

Alina Vitukhnovskaya on Russia 1996

♦ The Association of American Publishers, the American Booksellers Association and the American Library Association take a page advertisement in the *New York Times* which states: 'Today is the publication date of Salman Rushdie's book *The Satanic Verses*: Free People Write Books, Free People Publish Books, Free People Sell Books,

Free People Buy Books, Free People Read Books. In the spirit of America's commitment to free expression we inform the public that this book will be available to readers at bookshops and libraries throughout the country'.

Fiction, Fact and the Fatwa: A Chronology of Censorship

♦ Without seeing the need for unlimited press freedom, one can perceive nothing.

Fyodor Dostoevsky

♦ Article 19's plainspoken promise of freedom of 'information and ideas' for all provides the perfect umbrella text for those of us in the press freedom business.

♦ The prosecutions and censorship of journalists are justified by governments under the terms of the 'other' Article 19: Article 19 of the International Covenant of Civil and Political Rights. The ICCPR version of Article 19 restates the basic free-expression promise of its progenitor and then buries it under a cascade of caveats, exemptions and pretexts for government interference in the media.

Bill Orme 1998

♦ It is more than ever important that the evil of censorship should be explained by reference to principles which are likely to be acceptable outside free-thinking and liberal circles.

♦ It seems unwise to expect that the right to free expression of feeling and of opinion in art and literature will be universally accorded some overriding, or at least very high, priority. Therefore one still has to look for principles that are at least widely acceptable across frontiers, and across different moralities, and which entail the paramount necessity of free expression, even when viewed from different and opposing moral standpoints.

Stuart Hampshire 1992

♦ Is freedom of speech a universal human right? Or is it, after all, just one value among others, a value cherished by middle-class intellectuals in Western democracies, but one which other cultures, drawing on different traditions, might well reject as unsuitable for them, and which radical groups within those Western democracies might well challenge as no longer central even there?

Ronald Dworkin 1994

♦ Freedom of speech, which is quite unnecessary to most people's individual ambitions for themselves, has nothing to do with selfishness. It is, however, indispensable to the most basic, organic, social responsibility a people can have, which is the responsibility together to decide, in response if not in formal elections, what their collective political values really are.

Ronald Dworkin 1997

♦ Freedom of speech is almost constantly under threat, not just in dictatorships but in democracies as well, and we must struggle to defend it at almost any cost.

Ronald Dworkin 2002

♦ Speech is more uninhibited, robust and wide open than it has ever been in the US, more so than in any country on earth.

Anthony Lewis 1995

♦ What is already clear is that civil liberties, the right of the citizen to dissent, tolerance of others' opinions, polite debate, freedom of expression and all sorts of legal protections are under threat as a direct result of 11 September 2001 and the war on terrorism.

Phillip Knightley on the US 2002

♦ If the people of a country choose to live like human beings, choose happiness and beauty, their way lies first through universal human rights and then through universal, unlimited freedom of thought. The people of countries that have opposed this will enter the twenty-first century without honour.

Yasar Kemal 1995

♦ Whenever a country considers itself to be at war, freedom of expression is the first casualty. The urge to abandon plurality and debate is overwhelming.

Freimut Duve 2002

♦ Deprived of one's freedom of expression a man can easily lapse into despair, accept this unfreedom as his inevitable fate, fall silent and give up his soul to darkness – on the other hand, he can see this as a challenge. He may then discover that his earlier, more public, existence had been a form of escape from his own self, that while he was always ready to hold up a mirror to the world at large, he himself avoided looking in it or looked into a less harsh and critical one. And so today I believe that it is less important for a writer to worry about his freedom of expression than about what it is he wants to express. Or to put it another way: that he should at all times endeavour to express himself as a dignified, incorruptible and free human being.

Ivan Klíma 1981

♦ The murder of Manuel de Dios provides brutal proof, if proof were needed, that freedom of speech is no mere abstraction. Writers and journalists, who insist upon this freedom and see in it the world's best weapon against tyranny and corruption, know also that it is a freedom which must constantly be defended, or it will be lost. Those they write against – drug dealers, political tyrants, religious despots – also understand the power of free expression all too well, and go to terrible lengths to suppress it.

Salman Rushdie 1992

♦ The triumph of Islam in the seventh century AD led not to the suppression of aboriginal Arabic traditions but simply to their being forgotten. The great originals of pre-Islamic poetry were swept away as if by floodwater.

Peter Porter and Harriet Harvey-Wood 1997

♦ For the West, and in many ways for us, freedom of expression is a 'sacred cow' – even when the books do get cooked sometimes.

Vitaly Tretyakov 2000

♦ In April 1994, the German constitutional court declared that denials of the Holocaust are not protected by free speech.

♦ I know how strong the case for censorship seems in Germany now; I know that decent people are impatient with abstract principles when they see hoodlums with pseudo-swastikas pretending that the most monumental, cold-blooded genocide ever was the invention of its victims. The hoodlums remind us of what we often forget: the high, sometimes nearly unbearable, cost of freedom.

Ronald Dworkin on Germany 1995

FREEDOM

♦ There is no place on this earth where a man might be totally free. Nor can I imagine a force that would be capable of permanently depriving people of all freedom. Contemporary society cannot exist in complete freedom, nor can it exist in complete unfreedom.

♦ And so, as I have said, it is his inner freedom that really counts where an artist is concerned. He can live and work surrounded by brutality, he can live and work even though deprived of his rights. After all, the great Russian literature of the nineteenth century was created in one of the most unfree empires the world has ever known. Dostoyevsky was sentenced to death, and he lived in prisons and in exile. Solzhenitsyn conceived his works – at least in his mind – while serving time in the labour camps of Siberia. Many great works have only come to be published after the death of their author. But no worthwhile work can be created by someone who lacks internal freedom.

♦ I would say that it is the man who knows how to choose, to detect his very own opportunity at every decisive turn in his life, who is truly internally free; he is not afraid of that voice, should it ever speak to him.

♦ The internal freedom of each and every one of us will doubtless reveal itself in the way in which we are capable of discovering and maintaining this most fundamental aim of life, the way we again and again endeavour to keep faith with it, not allowing any external influence or pressure to divert us from it – whether this pressure takes the form of fashion, trend, convention, ideology, success, police terror, or the corrupting effect of fame and wealth.

♦ That is not to say that the road to freedom necessarily leads via some kind of asceticism. Nor would I claim that one has to come into conflict with the powers-that-be in order to gain internal freedom. No, all I am trying to say is that these two categories – external freedom, which allows one to accept all the joys and privileges (but also disadvantages) of modern life, and genuine internal freedom – have very little to do with on another.

Ivan Klíma 1981

♦ Just as the notion that the end of the Cold War and the collapse of the Soviet system would lead to a new age proved to be naive, so has the hope that the democratic process by itself must automatically guarantee the basic freedoms. During the 1980s, country after country in Latin America gave up military dictatorship in favour of freely elected government. Yet, in several countries, the instinct for repression has lingered on, and so has the instinct for acting beyond the law.

John Simpson 1993

♦ Those conditions of life we regard as essential to freedom and prosperity we see as open and visible, and those which are occluded, oppressive and secret we judge to be in shadow. The so-called free nations are not properly free while the oppressing nations go on being truly oppressive.

Peter Porter and Harriet Harvey-Wood 1997

♦ The word 'freedom' is of course an abstraction, and people today are probably weary of it.

Stephen Spender 1972

♦ I used to be an independent critic of politicians, looking in from the outside; then I became a politician myself. Nevertheless, I believe freedom should always be given priority.

Václav Havel 2002

♦ No one really wants another revolution. But definitely everybody wants an evolution toward more social freedom.

Shiva Kambari on Iran 2002

♦ There have been ominous signs that our fragile liberties have been dramatically at risk since the 1970s when the white-shirt-and-tie FBI re-invented itself from a corps of 'generalists' trained in law and accounting into a confrontational 'Special Weapons and Tactics' (aka SWAT) Green Beret-style army of warriors who like to dress up in camouflage or black ninja clothing and, depending on the caper, the odd ski mask.

Gore Vidal on the US 2002

FREEDOM OF INFORMATION

♦ The Right claims that an individual can better exercise freedom of choice by being economically liberated through the market. Yet, unlike its counterpart in the USA, the British government continues to control information. It has maintained legislation restricting the 'promotion' of gay and lesbian lifestyles, and established the Broadcasting Standards Council to preview and 'maintain' standards in television.

Mark Fisher 1995

♦ If a government feels threatened by being open and implements freedom of information legislation reluctantly or cautiously, little will change. What we need is a government which believes that in the long term freedom of information will lead to better decision making.

♦ If there had been a Freedom of Information Act on the UK statute book, would the British people have been better informed about arms to Iraq or Bovine Spongiform Encephalopathy (BSE)?

Mark Fisher 1996

♦ The freedom of information promised by direct satellite broadcasting is being thwarted by media monopolies and broadcasters' willingness to accommodate reactionary governments.

Christopher Hird 1994

♦ How do we discover what government, or companies, do not want to tell us? The obstacles are great: we have no Freedom of Information Act.

Maurice Frankel 1995

G

GENOCIDE

GLOBALISATION

GOVERNMENT

GENOCIDE

♦ The Genocide Convention is the simplest and starkest of all international instruments. Without any qualification or ambiguity it demands that states prevent and punish the crime of genocide. Killing in war might be acceptable – including killing civilians in certain (in fact rather many) circumstances – but genocide is completely beyond the pale.

♦ The requirement of the Genocide Convention is simple and overriding. Law can only spell out the obligation, it is for human morality and ingenuity to do the rest.

Alex de Waal 1998

♦ My generation grew up with the idea that after World War II, such a war with its genocide, concentration camps and forced resettlement of entire populations was simply not possible. I no longer believe Europe has learned that lesson.

Slavenka Drakulic on the Balkans 2001

GLOBALISATION

♦ Economically, globalisation occurs according to the demands of capital. Where do the poor fit into the process?

Leonardo Boff 1999

♦ Our world is today falling under the influence of a new form of governmental power that has destabilising effects upon democracies everywhere. This new polity can be called cosmocracy. The political system of cosmocracy is far 'messier' and self-contradictory than most people yet realise. It defies the simplifications and confusions of prevailing theories of 'globalisation' that think in the old-fashioned terms of (potentially) 'sovereign' territorial states or 'multi-level governance'.

♦ In discussions of the system of global governance (cosmocracy) the word 'system' commonly comes in for a battering. It is often greeted with puzzlement, or outright derision, mainly because the tangled mess of governmental and para-governmental institutions that have global effects seem to defy description, let alone political judgement. This so-called global system of governance seems to be a global system of anarchy: it seems that no institution or body regularly occupies the seats of power. Its complex and contradictory logic seems to be *sauve qui peut*. It is as if there are no secure rules or regulations; nobody seems to be in charge. Little wonder, then, that most languish in its presence. It seems to defy description, and so to induce a feeling of faintness, even fatalism, before the powers that be. This fatalism is the enemy of democracy. Its horns need to be grasped, initially by understanding better how it works. The fatalist, who comes in two types, is generally someone who feels overwhelmed or overpowered by the world. One of them, the ignoramus, is simply ignorant, and confident in that ignorance, often supremely so in the straightforward conclusions that are drawn. He or she knows all right who rules the world: it is the rich and powerful, or the big multinational corporations, or the United States of America, for instance. And that's that.

John Keane 2002

GOVERNMENT

♦ The sin of Power is to not only distort reality but to convince people that the false is true, and that what is happening is only an invention of enemies.

Arthur Miller 1978

♦ There are three other categories where governments do practise, or at least attempt to apply, censorship. These are administrative convenience; public reputation (of ministers or officials); and personal embarrassment.

Alan Clark 1995

♦ The creation of state publishing institutions represents a subtle form of state censorship. While commercial publishers are not barred from publishing school textbooks, even when these are acceptable, they can only be used as supplementary or reference materials.

Henry M Chakava on Kenya 1996

H

HATE SPEECH

HISTORY

HUMAN RIGHTS

HUMOUR

HATE SPEECH

♦ Any advocacy of national, racial or religious hatred that constitutes incitement to discrimination, hostility or violence must be prohibited.

International Covenant on Civil and Political Rights: Article 20

♦ Those concerned with freedom of expression have been understandably wary of restrictions on 'hate speech', generally taking the view that obnoxious and intolerant opinions are best combated by more speech rather than by censorship. In any case, restrictive laws rarely have the intended effect.

Richard Carver and Adewale Maja-Pearce 1995

♦ But we can't fight imagination's dark side by suppressing what has come to be called 'hate speech', we cannot drive the fantasies of bigotry underground and give paranoid hatred a comforting dose of martyrdom and darkness to hide its insecurities.

AL Kennedy 2002

♦ The most dangerous threat behind hate speech is surely that it can go beyond its immediate targets and create a *culture of hate*, a culture which makes it acceptable, respectable even, to hate on a far wider scale. Such a culture of hate is not easy to define, and does not necessarily have one trajectory, but its evolution is evident in the circumstances surrounding some events in recent history. Words can turn into bullets, hate speech can kill and maim, just as censorship can.

Ursula Owen 1998

♦ If Rwandan crimes against humanity ever come to trial, the owners of Radio des Mille Collines (RTLM) will stand at the head of the accused.

♦ 'One Belgian each' was the slogan adopted by RTLM. Instructions allegedly broadcast by RTLM included information on the handling of grenades and different methods of killing the 'enemy' – Tutsis, opposing Hutus and Belgians.

François Misser and Yves Jaumain on Rwanda 1994

♦ The reason the media were so effective in inciting violence in Rwanda and Yugoslavia is precisely that they had an exclusive capacity to communicate. The violence that was incited was inextricably linked to the broadcasts.

Aryeh Neier 1998

♦ The powerful and painful paradox of laws against hate speech is that again and again they have been turned against the very people we would see as victims of that hate speech. In Eastern Europe and the former Soviet Union, laws against defamation and insult were used to persecute crimes of the Communist regimes. In Turkey the law was used against Ismail Besikci, Turkish scholar, for his writings on human rights abuses against the country's Kurdish population. The South African laws against racial hatred under apartheid were used systematically against the victims of the state's racist policies.

Ursula Owen 1998

HISTORY

♦ The biggest opportunities for rewriting history now are in the former Communist world, where topics have emerged from taboo and formerly proscribed versions are being rebuilt from the rubble. In a recent edition of the standard Hungarian historical atlas for schools, the 'Liberation of our Homeland' has been re-labelled 'Military Operations in Hungary, 1944–5'.

♦ The Moravian Empire, the greatness of Lithuania in the late Middle Ages, the role of Free Polish forces in World War II are among subjects newly risen or restored to prominence in the historiography of their own countries. 'National' heroes are being re-elevated or invented: Genghis Khan in Mongolia, Alexander the Great in Macedonia, Gjerje Fishta in Albania, János Hunyadi in Hungary.

♦ While we wait for the rest of the world to catch Europe's devolutionary virus, marginalised and minoritarian groups and regions are getting the benefit of some of the historical attention formerly grabbed by metropolis, empire and state. The fashion for world history helps. World history, to me, is what happens at the edges, where cultures and civilisations, like tectonic plates, scrape against each other and set up seismic effects. Admittedly, the project of rehabilitating the overlooked seems sometimes to become just another way of piling up metropolitan history, because what gets recorded and transmitted is usually selected according to the centre's criteria of importance.

♦ Children, women, the socially underprivileged, the sick, the 'mad' and the ethnic minorities have had to wait for elite perceptions to change before getting historians of their own.

♦ As well as by political change, historical revisionism is being stimulated by science. Historians, who formerly tried to crush the facts to fit procrustean models and schemes, are beginning to enjoy the respectability of uncertainty. History is coming to be avowed as chaotic: a turbulence which happens at random or in which causes are often, in practice, impossible to trace; or a state of near-equilibrium, punctuated – like evolution, according to a current theory – by spasmodic change.

♦ Even as history succumbs to the influence of science, it is becoming less 'scientific' in the conventional sense. Out of structuralism and post-structuralism, a new humanism has evolved that relishes texts as evidence of themselves rather than as means to reconstruct events.

♦ Heroes come and go, history marches on, written and rewritten to fit the needs of the time and the exigencies of political propaganda.

♦ Thanks to a healthy Pyrronist revival, this millennium is twitching to a close amid doubts about whether an objectively true version of the past even exists to be recovered: history, after all, happened to people who experienced it variously at the time, registered it mentally in contrasting patterns and recorded it in mutually contradictory ways.

Felipe Fernández-Armesto 1995

♦ Resistance to historical truth is a function of group identity: nations and peoples tie their sense of themselves into narcissistic narratives which strenuously resist correction.

♦ For what seems apparent in the former Yugoslavia, in Rwanda and in South Africa is that the past continues to torment because it is *not* past.

♦ Nations, properly speaking, cannot be reconciled to other nations, only individuals to individuals. Nonetheless, individuals can be helped to heal and to reconcile by public rituals of atonement.

♦ If, instead of writing books niggling at the numbers exterminated at Jasenovac, President Franjo Tudjman of Croatia had gone to the site of the most notorious of the Croatian extermination camps and publicly apologised for the crimes committed by the Croatian *Ustashe* against Serbs, gypsies, Jews and partisans, he would have liberated the Croatian present from the hold of the *Ustashe* past.

♦ The experience of the war in Yugoslavia makes it difficult to conceive of reconciliation, if it were ever possible, in terms of those clichés 'forgiving and forgetting', 'turning the page', 'putting the past behind us' and so on.

♦ But reconciliation might eventually be founded on something starker: the democracy of the dead, the equality of all victims, the drastic nullity of all struggles that end in killing and the demonstrable futility of avenging the past in the present.

Michael Ignatieff 1996

♦ It was a Hungarian historian who said that in this part of the world 'the past is never idle'.

WL Webb 1994

♦ Only through the cracks in the official version do we find the human actors who are the real stuff of any history.

Urvashi Butalia 1997

♦ The historical narrative we were taught in school, with its emphasis on partition and freedom, did not accentuate or define, in my mind, my parents' experiences and lives, and my own place as a child of people displaced from their homeland; if anything, it suppressed such formulations.

Amit Chaudhuri on India 1997

♦ In all societies, the past is continuously adapted and revised to reflect shifts in current ideology and political agenda.

♦ The astonishing shifts in US foreign policy are less post-modern than textbook Orwellian: last year's ally and favoured arms customer (whether Saddam, Mobutu or Noriega) becomes today's enemy; today's 'emerging democracy' was last year's terrorist state.

Stanley Cohen 2000

♦ Historians are dangerous, and capable of turning everything topsy-turvy. They have to be watched.'

Nikita Khruschev in 1956, quoted in *Index* 1995

♦ 'Stalin ... started the prodigious falsification of history which was to descend like a destructive avalanche upon Russia's intellectual horizon.'

Isaac Deutscher 1995

♦ Over the following centuries the black legend, just as much as the pink legend, multiplied the misunderstandings which marked America's entrance into western history. The two poles of this opposition – this false opposition – leave us outside true history, which has little or nothing to do with the history written by, and for, the victors.

♦ The black legend asks us to enter the Museum of the Good Savage, where we can shed tears over the obliterated happiness of a few wax figures that have nothing in common with the flesh-and-blood beings who people our lands. The pink legend, on the other hand, invites us into the Great Temple of the West where we can add our voices to the

Universal Choir, intoning hymns in celebration of Europe's great civilising mission, to conquer the world in order to save it.

Eduardo Galeano 1995

♦ Many in the older generation of academics, themselves responsible for the founding myths, accuse the new historians of destroying the foundations of the state and threatening its legitimacy.

♦ Benny Morris, an historian in the classic mould and a compulsive digger in the archives, failed to play by the rules of the academic establishment and was stigmatised as a 'revisionist' in the same negationist category as, for instance, Robert Faurisson, who denies the Shoah.

Baruch Kimmerling on Israel 1995

HUMAN RIGHTS

♦ 'Everyone is entitled to a social and international order in which the rights and freedoms set forth in the [UDHR] declaration can be fully realised.'

Article 28

♦ 'Everyone has the right to respect for his private and family life, his home and his correspondence.'

Article 8

♦ 'Everyone has the right to freedom of thought, conscience and religion; this right includes freedom to change his religion or belief, and freedom, either alone or in community with others and in public or private, to manifest his religion or belief, in worship, teaching, practice and observance'.

Article 9

♦ 'Everyone has the right to freedom of expression. This right shall include freedom to hold opinions and to receive and impart information

an ideas without interference by public authority and regardless of frontiers. This article shall not prevent States from requiring the licensing of broadcasting, television or cinema enterprises.'

Article 10

♦ 'Everyone has the right to freedom of peaceful assembly and to freedom of association with others, including the right to form and to join trade unions for the protection of his interests.'

Article 11

European Convention on Human Rights, Rome 1950–Strasbourg 1966

♦ From the proposition that one has a right to do something it does not follow that it is a right or even morally permissible thing to do.

John Searle 1996

♦ In the name of fighting fundamentalism, human rights are becoming the first casualty as Arab governments seize the pretext to curb all their dissidents.

Caroline Moorehead 1996

♦ In the quest for foreign markets, many professed commitments to human rights are being forgotten.

Caroline Moorehead and Ursula Owen 1996

♦ Human rights reached its high point this century in 1989. Communism had been defeated and with it the ferocious suppression of Eastern European dissidents: the Berlin wall was down. It lasted no more than a few months.

♦ The recent history of human rights is marked by swings between those who maintain that major powers like America have a duty to intervene to promote freedom, democracy and self-determination, and those who believe that states should mind their own business.

Caroline Moorehead 1997

♦ It would make for a more lucid debate if we dropped the language of rights and values, and simply talked about politics.

Ian Buruma 1997

HUMOUR

♦ What the joke reveals is inconsistency. The joke is all the time exposing points of vulnerability, where the personality or the regime cannot sustain itself, and that is where the danger is. Anything in a regime that you can laugh at is likely to be a point of contention: wherever there's laughter, there's the debate that's being suppressed, the conflict that can't be opened up. A joke is like a diagnosis. Wherever in the system you can be amused, you've touched on something that cannot be discussed.

♦ When you live in an oppressive system, by definition the system works to stop you having certain thoughts. Once you are able to be in an ironic position, it is as though you have found another place from which you can think about something.

♦ Humourlessness is a defence. But I think humour is the last thing before violence. I think there's something good about the wish to change things through persuasion, of which humour is a kind. There's a great fear about what happens when the humour breaks down, because once humour breaks down, you have nothing left. It would be optimistic to say that all you've got to do is laugh and the regime comes tumbling down, but it would be equally naive to assume that humour has no power. Once people begin to see the absurd side of things, things feel less terrifying. It is almost like psychic alchemy. There's this terrifying person or regime, and you have to find ways of looking at them or describing them so that you can do more with them. If you can be amused, or render them absurd or surreal in some way, it is as though you've then got more imaginative space inside you to look at them. I think that is what people are looking for.

Adam Phillips 2000

♦ If you like, satire is tolerated as a safety valve by democratic politicians, as just another humiliation to suffer along with having to prostitute themselves in order to win advancement. With this safety valve, we are thus prevented from all going mad at the insupportable horror of everything. All in all, it's a small price to pay.

♦ Satire is never dead, and its effectiveness can be gauged by the response of the satirised. The great British twentieth-century cartoonist David Low was generally recognised during World War II as one of the most effective anti-Nazi propagandists because, rather than rendering the Nazis as sinister (which they certainly were) he made them, to quote a Tory MP at the time, 'look like bloody fools'. It got Low on to the Gestapo death list, which is praise indeed. Then again, the last cartoonist to be imprisoned in Britain was the cartoonist for *Bulldog*, the newspaper of the fascist British Movement, who was sent down in the mid-eighties for incitement to racial hatred. And we're back to Hitler's jokes, and the moral neutrality of humour.

♦ I assume that those people who consider political correctness to be the greatest tyranny we currently strain under have just forgotten to say that, actually, they want a return to their previously untrammelled freedom to call blacks niggers, Jews Yids, gays poofs and women whores; and if any of those groups object, it's simply because they 'can't take a joke'.

♦ Although I don't find jokes made by the powerful about the powerless particularly funny, nor the way the powerful have and will silence and often murder the powerless for making jokes about them, maybe it's just the way they tell them.

Martin Rowson 2000

♦ Lenny Bruce's satire was his way of responding to a culture wallowing in its own hypocrisy. If it was considered sick to have a photo of him picnicking in a cemetery on the cover of his first album, he knew it as really sicker to enforce racial segregation of the bodies that were allowed to be buried in that cemetery.

Paul Krassner 2000

♦ Against the assault of laughter nothing can stand.

Mark Twain, quoted in *Index* 2000

♦ Israel's former defence minister, Moshe Dayan, put it somewhat differently: 'I would not fear the Egyptians even if they possessed nuclear weapons. But I will begin to feel nervous when they stop making jokes about themselves and about others'. The underlying meaning is that the society that doesn't laugh could explode at any minute.

Saeed Okasha 2000

♦ Severe but lesser sanctions against cartoonists and those who publish them have included floggings and long terms of imprisonment. In 1992, Manouchehr Karimzadeh was sentenced by Iran's revolutionary court to 50 lashes, one year in prison and a fine of 500,000 rials for a cartoon the authorities claimed bore an unacceptably close resemblance to Ayatollah Khomeini and appeared to have a hand missing – a reference to Islamic-style punishment.

Mark Nesbit 2000

♦ In alternative comics, making people laugh can be a dangerous business.

Roger Sabin 2000

♦ Anything in a regime that you can laugh at is likely to be a point of contention: wherever there's laughter, there's the debate that's being suppressed, the conflict that can't be opened up. A joke is like a diagnosis. Wherever in the system you can be amused, you've touched on something that cannot be discussed.

Art Spiegelman 2000

I

IDENTITY

♦ The main hope of harmony in the contemporary world lies not in any imagined uniformity but in the plurality of our identities, which cut across each other and work against sharp divisions around one uniquely hardened impenetrable faultline. The political leaders who dispute the clash of civilisations but think and act in terms of a unique partitioning of humanity into 'the western world', 'the Muslim world', 'the Hindu world', and so on, make the world not only more divisive but also much more flammable. They also end up privileging the voice of religious authorities (who become the *ex officio* spokesmen), while muffling other voices and silencing other concerns.

♦ The robbing of our plural identities not only reduces us, it impoverishes the world.

Amartya Sen 2002

♦ As history demonstrates, prohibitions of language, religion, identity and thought represent deeper moral and ethical blows to a country than economic crises and natural disasters.

Mehmed Uzun on Turkey 2001

♦ The political changes which dethroned communist regimes have also broken up big states, especially in Europe, where some peoples have recovered or are reasserting ancient identities. Some have attained devolution, autonomy or independence; others are calling or fighting for it. The agglutinative high-politics of Brussels, say, or Moscow, struggle with the amoeba-like micro-politics of the Caucasus or the Pyrenees. Disintegration is happening at the same time as integration. In consequence, instead of history written to legitimate empires and nation-states, we are now getting 'devolutionist' histories, addressed to a world of subsidiarity.

Felipe Fernández-Armesto 1995

♦ But nations are not like individuals: they do not have a single identity, conscience or responsibility. National identity is a site of conflict and argument, not a silent shrine for collective worship.

Michael Ignatieff 1996

♦ Prospective or actual loss of identity is the core anxiety agitating the new lost tribes of Europe.

Nicholas Fraser 2001

INDEX ON CENSORSHIP

♦ The goal that *Index* still pursues can be described as the embarrassment of tyranny, wherever it appears. Embarrassment is not the most dramatic of sentiments, and the sensations associated with it are not as violent as with shame. But while well-established tyrants, whether an individual, an ethnic group or a party, are unlikely to feel shame, they are likely to suffer political and personal embarrassment, which is a social sentiment, when they go out into the world and meet their peers – even if, like the governments of the Soviet Union and of South Africa, they are for a long time sustained by their belief in the God-given, or history-given, righteousness of their cause. Probably economic pressures are always the strongest pressures, but public embarrassment certainly has a part to play.

♦ Suppose we now assume that the 'glare' of publicity (the metaphor, however hackneyed, is a good one) from now onwards can be switched to any part of the world where the denial of free expression in its grosser forms still survives, or where it comes into being. Stories of the imprisonment of dissidents, and of the suppression of books and newspapers and works of art, will become very widely known through the efforts of *Index* and others. It will become more and more difficult to conceal from the rest of the world that the common decencies of humanity are in specific countries being ignored.

Stuart Hampshire 1992

INTERNET

♦ The internet necessitates a review of the right of free speech.

Simon Davies 1997

♦ In the new dimension of cyberspace, real freedom is at last possible. A virtual world of true democracy where no speaker is more powerful than any other has been created, unplanned and unsanctioned by the potentates of telecommunications and computing. A world, moreover, that appears to be, to all intents and purposes, free and unregulated. 'A consequence of unleashing the power of individual activity', according to the *Economist*. This is specious nonsense.

Brian Winston and Paul Walton 1996

♦ [UK minister of education David] Blunkett said: 'We all share a responsibility to make sure that children's use of the internet is appropriate and safe. Suppliers are also expected to offer adequate filtering of the material which can be accessed through their connections to the internet.' To the student of historical attempts at censorship key words leap out: 'unsuitable', 'appropriate'. To the observer of internet censorship one word looms frighteningly large: 'filtering'.

Frank Fisher on the UK 2000

♦ The commercial future of the internet depends on a universally-accepted and foolproof method of on-line identification; as of now, the only means of providing it is through strong encryption.

♦ The FBI and the National Security Agency (NSA) have instigated efforts to restrict the availability of encryption worldwide.

David Banisar and Simon Davies 1998

♦ It is wrong to talk about the internet spreading democracy: in most non-democratic countries, most people have never made a phone call.

Simon Kuper 2002

◆ What if cyberspace turns out to be just a holding tank for a new mass of believers? Believers who *think* that they are part of a community, who *think* that they are sincere ('best thought, first thought', Allen Ginsberg) but, in effect, are just extorted of time, energy and body by an imaginary space owned by alien military forces (ie ours)?

◆ The real American century would thus be replaced by the virtual American century, a bloodless and a gutless place where even wars can be fought from a distance from your home computer, without once seeing the faces of your victims but seeing, rather, the happy faces of *Techne*, the always-smiling Virtuality.

◆ The human idiom is limited while machine idiom is UNLIMITED. The interactive idiom may turn out to be a one-way conversation: the tireless machine will keep talking while the exhausted human will fall silent.

Andrei Codrescu 1995

◆ Anonymity on the internet is not a thorny issue; it is a constitutional right.

◆ An end to internet anonymity would chill free expression in cyberspace and strip away one of the key structural privacy protections enjoyed by internet users.

ACLU (American Civil Liberties Union) 2000

◆ The invisible hand of cyberspace is building an architecture that is quite the opposite of what it was at cyberspace's birth. The invisible hand, through commerce, is constructing an architecture that perfects control.

◆ When we see the path that cyberspace is on, we see that much of the 'liberty' present at cyberspace's founding will vanish in its future. Values that we now consider fundamental will not necessarily remain. Freedoms that were foundational will slowly disappear.

Lawrence Lessig 2000

♦ The implication is that the internet in 2005, say – let us call it Net2005 – could look very different from the internet as it was in 1995. The old, libertarian layer will still exist, but a new layer – the e-commerce stratum – will sit above it. And the values implicit in the architecture of this new layer will be radically different from those implicit in the old one.

♦ The key difference will be that the new layer will use the technical facilities of the old layer to eliminate anonymity and erode privacy. To understand how this will happen, you have to know something about how the net operates.

♦ The decentralised, permissive structure of the net is what gives it its resilience and what has enabled it to spread like a virus through society.

♦ Cyberspace – the most gloriously open, uncensored and unregulated public space in human history – could easily become the most controlled environment imaginable.

♦ Governments have traditionally been ambivalent about the internet. On the one hand, they desire the economic benefits that it brings. On the other, they are deeply apprehensive about its accountability.

John Naughton 2000

♦ The net is, fundamentally, about free speech . . . It poses a fundamental threat not only to the authority of the government but to all authority.

♦ Sakharov argued that prosperity requires access to information, and information widely spread is a great deterrent to tyranny.

Matthew Hoffman 1994

♦ The web is emerging as an organising medium, a way for activists of all stripes and on all continents to mobilise constituencies and galvanise political action.

Danny Schechter 2000

♦ Concerned mothers want new regulations on the internet and other forms of expression in the interests of their children that would restrict free speech for all.

Salil Tripathi on the US 2000

INTERROGATION

♦ I should state in addition to my former evidence that I also read the above-named counter-revolutionary poem 'We are alive but no longer feel the land beneath our feet' to Narbut, VI. When he heard this poem Narbut said to me, 'This never happened,' which must mean that I shouldn't tell anyone that I had read this poem to him.

♦ I admit that I am guilty of being the author of a counter-revolutionary satire against the leader of the Soviet Communist Party and the Soviet country. I request that I be allowed to write down separately this satire and add it to the present record of the interrogation.

Osip Mandelstam under interrogation by KGB in 1934, 1991

♦ In May 1938 the poet Osip Emilyevich Mandelstam was arrested. This second arrest was completely unexpected. It is unclear to me how the investigation into Mandelstam's counter-revolutionary activity was conducted if I – who as a result of his illness did not go a step away from him for many years – was not brought into the investigation as a participant or witness. I add that at the time of his arrest in 1934 Mandelstam was suffering from acute psychosis, moreover the investigation and exile developed during his illness. At the time of his second arrest, Mandelstam was seriously ill and both physically and mentally unstable.

Nadezhda Mandelstam letter to KGB in 1939, 1991

ISLAMOPHOBIA

♦ Islam has been feared and loathed by the West since it first made its appearance in Europe in the eighth century – within a century of its creation in the deserts of Arabia.

♦ While the term Islamophobia, coined to express the mix of fear and dread that characterises western attitudes to Islam, is of relatively recent date, modern anti-Muslim sentiment, as expressed in the British press, for instance, is simply one version of a well-established tradition more or less coterminous with the first confrontation of the two communities all those centuries ago.

♦ Then as now, the representation of 'the other' in a negative light legitimised existing power structures and served as propaganda in the long centuries of the battle against Islam.

♦ Muslims were – and still are – defined as barbaric, ignorant, closed-minded semi-citizens, or maddened terrorists and intolerant religious zealots.

♦ Today's Islamophobia feeds on history to fill out its stereotypes.

Tahir Abbas 2000

JOURNALISTS
JUSTICE

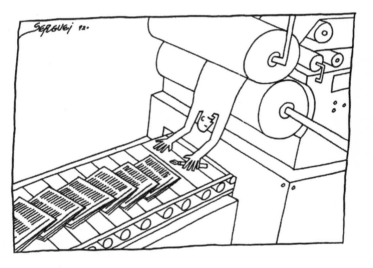

JOURNALISTS

♦ The intimidation and manipulation of journalists and publishers determine the news agenda. Journalists learn to avoid certain subjects or resort to a form of 'code' based on understatement and allusion to avoid crossing the tacit 'red lines'.

Samir Kassir 2000

♦ Journalists have never before been murdered in such numbers.

♦ For most of the dead journalists there are no histories, no obituaries: they are just names on a long list.

♦ The press has to take its share of the blame for genocide: too many journalists were in cahoots with murderers and kept a lid on what was going on.

Hervé Deguine and Robert Ménard on Rwanda 1994

♦ Adapting von Clausewitz, one can see journalism as the continuation of history by other means, a fairly desperate attempt to separate out from the racket of events what will still matter in a year's or a century's time.

WL Webb 1994

♦ For the latter part of September, October and most of November 2001 stories of people horribly incarcerated for minor offences caused not a ripple of concern because no journalist wanted to risk being labelled a 'terrorist sympathiser'.

♦ US journalists themselves have chosen self-censorship over that freedom of expression set out in the First Amendment.

Phillip Knightley 2002

♦ In the early afternoon of Wednesday 26 June this year Veronica Guerin, crime reporter for Ireland's *Sunday Independent*, was driving along the Naas dual carriageway at Clondalkin on the outskirts of Dublin. When

she stopped her car at traffic lights, a heavy white motorcycle drew alongside. Off jumped the helmeted pillion passenger, raised a handgun and, from just two feet away, shot Veronica five times in the chest and neck. He then climbed back on the bike which sped ahead and turned down a side road. By the time the police arrived, a most remarkable investigative reporter was dead.

♦ Paying tribute, her editor Aengus Fanning wrote of this darkest day in Irish newspaper history: 'For the first time a journalist has been murdered for daring to write about our criminal underworld and daring to chronicle the lives of the brutal people who inhabit it.' This was 'a blatant and terrifying attack on a free press and on freedom of speech'.

Martin Short 1996

♦ Journalists were and are necessary in a society where there was only limited forum for debate but where public opinion was always an important ingredient.

♦ Journalists, even when working for sectarian outlets, could demonstrate a professional detachment, allowing them to be viewed as somewhere between a necessary evil and a trusted conduit.

♦ Martin O'Hagan's death conforms to a worldwide trend, of which crime reporter Veronica Guerin's death outside Dublin a few years ago was a part. The most vulnerable journalist is a local journalist, not a star foreign correspondent wearing designer fatigues and body armour. The journalists most likely to be killed for their work are those whose revelations are read by those immediately affected within the community, not by an audience half a world away.

Michael Foley 2002

♦ The tape recorder is entirely to blame for the undue importance now attached to the interview . . . print media seems to share the erroneous idea that the voice of truth is not that of the journalist but of the interviewee.

♦ Perhaps the misfortune of schools of journalism is that while they do teach some useful tricks of the trade, they teach little about the profession itself.

Gabriel García Márquez 1997

♦ Journalists on dangerous assignments are considered civilians under article 79 of the Additional Protocol 1 of the Geneva Conventions, provided they do not do anything or behave in any way that might compromise this status, such as directly helping a war, bearing arms or spying. Any deliberate attack on a journalist that causes death or serious physical injury is a major breach of this Protocol and deemed a war crime.

RSF *Charter for the safety of journalists working in war zones or dangerous areas*

♦ Reporters Sans Frontières had the following statistics for 2002 (up to 29 November):

	2002	2001
Journalists killed	23	31
Media assistants killed	3	10
Journalists in prison	110	110
Media assistants in prison	3	11
Cyber-dissidents in prison	37	24

♦ In the early hours of 3 December, the four-storey printing facility of *Ozgur Ulke* newspaper in Istanbul was hit by a bomb which, in the words of its editor-in-chief Baki Karadeniz, left the building 'as if struck by an air raid'. The daily's editorial headquarters were simultaneously destroyed by a second bomb. In a third explosion some 200 miles away, *Ozgur Ulke*'s central office in Ankara was blown up. One newspaper worker was killed and 18 others injured.

RSF *Annual Report* 2002

♦ A total of 23 journalists were assassinated for writing for the two papers, *Ozgur Gundem* and *Ozgur Ulke*. Four reporters disappeared and only one tortured body, that of a reporter kidnapped by police, was found. By the end of 1995, 35 employees were serving prison terms, including every editor of the paper.

Ismet Imset on Turkey 1996

JUSTICE

♦ The Security Services Act of 1996 extends the powers of the intelligence services to carry out surveillance not only on known criminals, but also on people suspected of criminal acts or conspiracy.

Anon on the UK 1996

♦ The challenge for the tribunals is to prove that international justice can contribute to the creation of lasting peace in the aftermath of social breakdown.

♦ Supporters of the tribunals tend to say their fundamental contribution to reconciliation lies in the notion of individualising guilt.

Anthony Dworkin on War Crimes Tribunals 1996

♦ I asked Tom if countries always apologised when they had done wrong, and he says, 'Yes; the little ones does.'

Mark Twain, quoted in *Index* 1996

KILLING

KILLING

♦ 535 journalists killed in 10 years (totals for 2002 up to 5 November). 37% died because of differences of opinion with the authorities and for having denounced official corruption (13% of the total)

♦ **253 in war zones**

year	accidentally[1]	deliberately[2]
1992	10	6
1993	4	21
1994	21	73
1995	11	28
1996	0	9
1997	1	4
1998	1	2
1999	8	22
2000	4	5
2001	7	6
2002	3	7
TOTAL	70 (27%)	183 (73%)

[1] Killed by mortar fire, landmine explosion, bombing or shooting
[2] Killed in an attack or shooting of a journalist identified as such

◆ **282 outside war zones**

year	accidentally	deliberately for differences of opinion	deliberately for denouncing corruption
1992	17	24	6
1993	16	15	8
1994	3	33	4
1995	3	9	13
1996	12	9	6
1997	7	13	3
1998	7	12	1
1999	3	2	3
2000	7	5	11
2001	4	5	9
2002	2	3	7
TOTAL	81 (29%)	130 (46%)	71 (25%)

◆ **Areas of the world**

	totals	in war zones	outside war zones
Balkans	49	46	3
Chechnya	13	12	1
Sierra Leone	14	14	0
Algeria	60	60	0
Colombia	46	16	30
Rwanda	52	51	1
Afghanistan	10	10	0

Reporters Sans Frontières 2002

♦ 'I can only hope that by the time you read this, I will not be dead. My health has deteriorated badly and I have been denied access to my doctor, lawyer, family, newspapers etc these seven weeks of my detention. When the crunch came, a doctor from the military hospital in Port Harcourt was allowed to see me – just once. He made a recommendation which Lt-Col. Komo [Military administrator for Rivers State, which includes Ogoniland] refused to accept. In short, my murder is being officially planned and executed. The writ of *habeas corpus* we filed has come up four times. We have not been produced in court, so nothing can be done. After seven weeks, the police are yet to charge us to court which is what I need to clear my name. And the courts are going to recess soon.'

Ken Saro-Wiwa, executed by the Nigerian military 1996

♦ Nowhere has the new phrase 'censorship by the bullet' acquired more meaning than in Tajikistan, where civil war claimed at least 20,000 lives in six months in 1992, and in Turkey, where the continuing conflict between Kurds and the Turkish authorities has seen 12 journalists assassinated in 1993. *Ozgür Gündem,* a newspaper sympathetic to the Kurdish cause, started publication in May 1992. Since then, 16 of its journalists and distributors have been killed.

Caroline Moorehead 1994

♦ Nikolai Kluyev, one of the best poets in Russia, died while the First Congress of Soviet Writers was proceeding with pomp and ceremony in Moscow. Few writers spared a thought for Kluyev while welcoming the bright present and even brighter future, in which many of them would soon follow Kluyev to the scaffold.

♦ The KGB's victims died. Those who denounced them are still with us.

Vitaly Shentalinsky 1991

LANGUAGE

LAW

LIBERTY

LIBRARIES

LIES

139

LANGUAGE

♦ Some languages are more equal than others.

Davrell Tien 1994

♦ By some estimates, of the 7,000 or so languages spoken around the world, only 10% will still be there by the end of the 21st century. 'A language', goes the saying, 'is only a dialect with an army.' Of an estimated 300 languages spoken in the Americas when Columbus landed, only 175 are still spoken: of those, only 20 are being transmitted to the next generation. The anglophone web may be speeding up that process. There are those on the web who believe they can save or make nations by first saving their linguistic culture. Ultimately the founders of virtual nations, like most web users, really ought to get out more.

Rohan Jayasekera 2000

♦ To share a language with someone who considers you an enemy is no guarantee he will not try to eliminate you. I have not forgotten the German Jews, the Bosnian Muslims, so many people discriminated against because of their skin, their religion, their sexual preference, their tribal origins, massacred by men who speak their tongue, who long ago uttered the same nursery rhymes, who today lip-sync the same songs on the radio. What makes the other menacing could turn out to be precisely the fact that he or she partakes of our same syllables. Perhaps we kill the other because we fear that we could become him.

Ariel Dorfman 1997

♦ Language is so interwoven with every aspect of political, economic and institutional structures that one cannot decide on the basis of size which is most at risk.

Ned Thomas 2001

♦ Journalists in newly democratised Indonesia are striving to purge Bahasa of the detritus of euphemisms and military jargon instilled over three decades of authoritarian rule with a view to setting 'new standards for candour'. First for the chop are the terms 'pre-prosperity' for poverty, 'procedural error' for official corruption and 'rogue individual' for a member of a military death squad.

'In the news' 2000

♦ This world is a graveyard of wrecked languages and cultures. What cultures whose names and reputations we have never even heard have come and gone in this world? As a cultural mosaic, the cultures of Anatolia have been a source of modern cultures. If they had not tried to prohibit and destroy other languages and other cultures than those of the Turkish people, Anatolia would still make major contributions to world culture. And we would not remain as we are; a country half famished, its creative power draining away.

Yasar Kemal on Turkey 1995

♦ If we are going to play with language we must play extremely well.

♦ When other factors no longer exist, you're left facing only your language. I'd say a writer has a responsibility only to his language; he is not responsible for the 'motherland', or the 'people'.

Gao Xingjian 2002

♦ Because of its proven record in improving one's chances for survival and satisfaction, language has become a metaphor for a great many things that fall outside its purview.

Andrei Codrescu 1995

♦ The public use of Kurdish was banned until 1991. The mother language of an estimated 12 million Turkish citizens of Kurdish origin is now allowed, on paper. The Turkish media authority has allowed radio and TV broadcasts in the Kurdish language – but only by the minute. Kurdish radio broadcasts will be limited to a maximum of 45 minutes a day and 4 hours in total per week. Television will broadcast just 30 minutes per day and 2 hours maximum per week. Only the state broadcaster TRT may broadcast Kurdish programmes.

♦ Kurdish language courses can only be offered by private schools, just at weekends or during school holidays. Teachers must be Turkish citizens and hold an appropriate qualification. At present this is impossible because Kurdish at universities remains a banned subject.

Gill Newsham 2002

♦ Human beings make about 160 sounds. This, say linguists, is the sum of the vocal elements of all the world's languages. Some 5,000 languages or distinctive dialects faded away in the 20th century. In the Americas alone there are more than 1,000 languages that have disappeared or reached the brink of extinction in the past 30 years.

♦ Tribal people often say that to have stories about a land is to own it. The continuing voices, using the languages that carry the stories, that hold the knowledge, that sustain the links with the spirits, are a permanent challenge. A rival deed to the territory. They must be silenced.

Hugh Brody 1999

♦ Here I sit, without my mother's language, without my father's language. I am powerless. I only have Afrikaans. I am out. I feel sometimes like an exile. That, that is the sadness. Then you feel how painful that is, if you feel you are without the language. If I could have spoken it . . . but I couldn't. I can't.

Petrus Vaalboi, Bushman, 1999

♦ Kurdish, one of the ancient languages of Upper Mesopotamia that bears the mark of those civilisations, is my mother tongue. And Kurdish has been banned as the language of education and broadcasting for almost the entire history of the Turkish Republic [founded 1923]. Human beings do not have the freedom to choose their mother language but they are, nonetheless, responsible. I started to write Kurdish novels, despite the obstacles and prohibitions, because of an ethical and moral responsibility rather than any ideological or political motive.

Mehmed Uzun 2001

LAW

♦ 'All are equal before the law and are entitled without any discrimination to equal protection of the law.'

Universal Declaration of Human Rights Article 7

♦ There are no mysterious 'laws' or 'uncontrollable market forces' that we must silently obey, only decisions within human institutions that are subject to will and choice, as they have always been.

Noam Chomsky 1997

♦ James Madison had it right: the best press law is no press law.

Bill Orme 1998

♦ In the early part of this century press baron Lord Northcliffe defined the news as 'something someone, somewhere, wants to suppress; everything else is just advertising'.

Paul O'Connor 1998

♦ PII (Public Interest Immunity) certificates are a shockingly uncharted area of executive power which few senior officials – let alone ministers – seem to be familiar with.

♦ But it is the sheer power of these so-called 'gagging orders' that is most alarming.

Matthew D'Ancona on the UK 1994

♦ There are some 50 major pieces of legislation on the statute book in the UK whose effect, expressly or in practice, is to gag journalists.

♦ The latest example is the 1997 Protection from Harassment Act. In time, this could become a partial and back door Protection of Privacy Act.

♦ A cloud much larger than a man's hand hangs over the media in the shape of next year's Data Protection Bill, designed to implement by 1998 the corresponding European Union directive. The bill would turn the present Data Protection Registrar into a Commissioner with new powers to require those holding data to inform the individuals concerned what data is being held about them and why; and to introduce safeguards – like an obligation to obtain prior consent over the use of sensitive personal information – with wider compensation for those who can show that the regulations have been broken in their case. In its present form, the legislation would signal the end of any kind of investigative journalism in the UK.

Hugh Stephenson on the UK 1997

◆ Even if there are no 'censorship laws' as such, the UK has at its disposal a vast legal framework which allows the authorities to forbid or stop the publication or distribution of a lot of material – pictures, books, movies.

◆ Despite conflicting 'expert' evidence refuting the causal connection between video nasties and violent crime, the restrictions imposed by the home secretary Michael Howard are still in place.

◆ The British Board of Film Classification is empowered to ban films and videos; restrictions on television are numerous. According to the code of conduct established by the Independent Television Commission (ITC), The same code establishes strict controls on 'bad humour' and 'bad taste'. Advertising is constrained by clauses determining 'public decency'.

◆ It seems bizarre that the police have the power to decide what videos make suitable cases for prosecution: what qualifies them to be censors of pornographic videos from Sweden or Denmark? Should it really be the government who decided whether or not the British public may view a channel like 'Real Hot Dutch'?

◆ There are far more cut and censored films in the UK than in the rest of Europe; only Britain indulges in eccentricities like the Lady Chatterley trial; only in Britain would a director like Stanley Kubrick decide to censor by withdrawal his own movie (*A Clockwork Orange*) because he considered it unsuitable for this country.

◆ Some of the most powerful censorship in the UK is politically motivated. Under the Prevention of Terrorism Act, for instance, the

British government has near absolute power to stop publication or transmission of everything it deems too 'sensitive' on Northern Ireland. From 1988-1994 the home secretary's Broadcasting Ban was used to ban many documentary films, books, songs and silenced even the voices of supposed IRA members and sympathisers, on the troubles in Northern Ireland.

♦ The infamous 'D Notice Committee' can challenge at will whatever it considers a threat to national security.

♦ Over the years, British governments have developed a culture of secrecy that has now become a habit in day-to-day political life. Censorship is also used to cover up potential political scandals: anything threatening dangerous repercussions is not investigated.

♦ Censorship in the UK reveals a deeply conservative country still in thrall to its strict Protestant values. Not only does the state exercise powerful censorship, British society accepts, even demands in many instances, that it should do so.

♦ I am convinced that the powerful censorship operating in the UK is the outcome of the evolution of British society and politics over the last two centuries.

♦ Subjects like sex, for example, remain taboo because the establishment has always used 'moral values' as a means of controlling the rest of the population.

♦ As long as British society remains dominated by its class divisions or continues to tolerate the outrageous privileges of its royal family, it can expect censorship to remain as powerful as ever.

Fabrice Rousselot 1996

♦ Fear of libel actions serves as a constant reminder of the risk of publishing investigative journalism.

Philippa Nugent 1996

♦ Libel, government secrecy and the general climate still inhibit serious journalism in Britain, but less than they did 25 years ago. The 'D notice' system of self-censorship is in abeyance, and the Thatcher government overplayed its hand so badly in the Ponting case that the Official Secrets Act, too, is less of a threat. Libel is still a problem, all the more so because the popular press is now so disreputable that courts award even heavier libel damages than they used to.

Godfrey Hodgson 1995

♦ The UK has the world's most draconian libel laws. Welcome to London, libel capital of the world. The odds are overwhelmingly in favour of those who sue.

♦ If authors, editors or publishers have the smallest doubt that the truth of a proposition cannot be proven in court (even when in good faith), the story is usually dropped.

♦ In other countries some attempt is made to strike a balance between the right of free speech and the right to defend one's reputation. The Supreme Court observed that in free debate erroneous statements are inevitable and must be protected – otherwise free expression will not have the 'breathing space' it needs and media self-censorship will be inevitable.

♦ The press discharges vital functions as a bloodhound.

Helene Guldberg 2000

LIBERTY

♦ 'All human beings are born free and equal in dignity and rights. They are endowed with reason and conscience and should act towards one another in a spirit of brotherhood.'

Universal Declaration of Human Rights Article 1

♦ Too often we have, as a nation, sat in silence and watched as our liberties disappeared. There has been little sense of public outrage and only occasional spasmodic protest.

♦ Would we regain a positive sense of liberty if a future government stitched together the web of rights that has been undone over the past 15 years? If liberty is fully expressed by legal guarantees and rights, then the answer must be 'yes'. But in practice, many of our freedoms depend on an individual having the power or money to exercise them.

♦ We suffer from several peculiarly British vices: a sense of historic arrogance that breeds complacency and, above all, an over-developed and suffocating sense of deference – to those in authority, to those with money, to those with professional qualifications.

♦ Liberty, in the end, is a state of mind, not a gift of government.

Mark Fisher 1995

♦ They that can give up essential liberty to obtain a little temporary safety deserve neither liberty nor safety.

Benjamin Franklin, quoted in *Index* 2002

LIBRARIES

♦ The history of the libraries of antiquity quite often ends in flames.

Luciano Canfora 1999

♦ Man must not be stifled under paper. Perhaps the various burnings of the Alexandrian Library were necessary, like those Australian forest fires without which the new seeds cannot burst their shells and make a young, healthy forest.

William Golding 1999

Lost libraries of the twentieth century (a selection)

♦ **Poland** The Germans embarked on a policy of ruthless destruction of Polish libraries, archives and museums, including the National Library in Warsaw. The Germans formed 'Brenn-Kommandoes' (Arson Squads) to destroy Jewish books. Thus the great Talmudic Library of the Jewish Theological Seminary in Lublin was burned.

♦ **Germany** It has been estimated that a third of all German books were destroyed during World War II.

♦ **Pakistan** As a result of communal riots, two of the largest libraries of the Indian subcontinent in Lahore were damaged.

♦ **China** Following the communist takeover, libraries all over the country were purged of 'reactionary, obscene and absurd' publications.

During the Cultural Revolution, all libraries were closed for various lengths of time between 1966 and 1970. Some were closed permanently and burned. Others were thoroughly purged, only the books of Marx, Lenin and Mao being spared.

♦ **Tibet** In 1966, the Cultural Revolution wrought havoc in this Chinese-occupied territory. Red Guards invaded the leading monastery in Tibet and destroyed frescoes and irreplaceable historic manuscripts.

Compiled by Index **1999**

LIES

♦ What's clear is that our post-war disaster began with this lie we tell ourselves to hide from our history: the lie of innocence on the part of the perpetrators of atrocities, lies that have run on from one generation to the next.

Elfriede Jelinek on Austria 2000

♦ It seems that this culture of lies is something that the small nations of the Balkans created long ago, learning to live with it and reinforcing it to this day. Lying – just like dying, after all – has become a natural state, a norm of behaviour, liars are normal citizens. And if one really should give any credit to Dobrica Cosic, Serbian writer and failed president of the *false Yugoslavia*, then it must be for his remark: 'Lying is an aspect of our patriotism and confirmation of our innate intelligence.'

♦ 'When the homeland is at stake, I am prepared to lie,' said one Croatian journalist and she attained a high rating on the Croatian journalistic scene.

♦ The culture of lies is most easily established if we have an opponent who lies more than we do, or who speaks the ancient palindromic language, 'the devil's verse', the one that is read the same backwards and forwards, from left and right.

♦ One of the strategies by which the culture of lies is established is terror by forgetting (they force you to forget what you remember!). And terror by remembering (they force you to remember what you do not remember!).

Terror by remembering is a parallel process to terror by forgetting.

Dubravka Ugresic 1994

♦ Is there no distinction to be made between the words of those whose hate speech is a matter of conviction, however ignorant, deluded or prejudiced, and hate speech as propaganda, the calculated and systemic use of lies to sow fear, hate and violence in a population at large?

Ursula Owen 1998

♦ The great crimes of humanity are always backed by a great lie.

Ismaïl Kadare 1998

M

MADNESS

MEDIA

MEMORY

MIGRATION

MINORITIES

MULTICULTURALISM

MUSIC

MADNESS

♦ Politicising the mad and describing political dissidents in the language of mental health is pernicious. The mad are like the politically oppressed in so far as they can be the victims of a powerful consensus that needs to invalidate them.

♦ People are not called mad when sufficiently influential people agree with what they are saying.

♦ At worst the mad, like the politically dissident, are prevented from adding to the stock of available reality.

♦ It would be nicer and better if we stopped thinking in terms of reason and unreason, stopped working out who is mad and who is not, and started working out who we are prepared to listen to, and why; and, of course, what we imagine the consequences of such listening might be.

Adam Phillips 2001

♦ If what the mad say is nonsense and does not need to be heard, then anything that we would like to be nonsense and do not want to hear can, too easily, be named mad.

♦ There is widespread recognition of a history of using both mental health diagnosis (he is mad, so we can lock him up) and psychiatric treatment (she is mad, so we are curing her with mind-altering drugs/electric shock treatment/etc) as a form of censorship and silencing.

♦ The elaborate preparations made by the city of Genoa in the hope of containing protest at the 2001 G8 summit are well known. Rather less familiar is the use of psychiatric hospitals in the city's plan for containing any disorder.

Sara Maitland 2001

♦ In the USSR, they first declared their dissidents 'insane' and then locked them up in asylums to silence their voices.

Danny Schechter 2001

♦ If a variety of views were being expressed and heard in Rwanda, even the vilest radio station could not have incited a genocide in which 800,000 people were killed during a period of three months. If there had been an opportunity for other voices to have been heard in Serbia in the period when RTS and the nationalist press were monopolising communication, the influence of those voices would not have been so extreme.

Aryeh Neier 1998

♦ The Western media, which have often been influential in other fields of investigation, have been ineffective in breaking through this secrecy to report arms sales. And since anyone interested in controlling weapons must be concerned with using the media as a means of mobilising and channelling information – and also as a political platform for making the case for control – we need to understand why the media have been so reluctant.

Anthony Sampson 1991

♦ The stable of an effective Nigerian press is being constantly reduced through illegal closures by the police on orders from the military. Before long, even those who penetrate the iron curtain of Sani Abacha's militarised enclave will have no media through which to remind the Nigerian populace of the atrocities daily inflicted on their Ogoni compatriots.

Wole Soyinka 1994

♦ What else is happening in Turkey? God damn them, one is ashamed of being human. I will write this too. One morning a journalist friend of mine rang. We had worked together as journalists for years. 'Do you know what is going on?' he asked. 'What?' I replied. 'The police have taken away everyone who works for *Özgür Gündem* newspaper.' I immediately went to the newspaper offices and saw that police had cordoned off the building. I asked to go in but the police wouldn't let me. There was no one left to produce the newspaper. They had taken all

♦ Our enemies should recognise that we are crazed and unpredictable, with extraordinary destructive force at our command, so they will bend to our will in fear.

Noam Chomsky on the US 2000

MEDIA

♦ Sometimes it seems as if as many people want freedom from the media as freedom for it.

Danny Schechter 2000

♦ The media are indispensable conduits for disinformation, propaganda, half-truths and so forth.

♦ Except in totalitarian states, media are Janus-faced structures, straddling the frontier between State and civil society, looking both ways and feeding from both sources (not in equal measure).

♦ Fear engenders hatred and also fosters dependence on authority figures, the cult of whose personalities is celebrated and policed by the same media that disseminate the fear.

♦ Television is a pseudo-interactive medium, or *anti*-interactive, with a bag of tricks for disguising monologue as dialogue.

Mark Thompson 1999

♦ Foremost amongst the public goods which must be protected by government are the commitment to freedom of speech and diversity of view.

♦ Successive governments – of all political colours – have sought to protect those public goods by supporting public service broadcasting and by controlling the extent of media ownership.

♦ Regulation has both liberating and restricting aspects. Restricting when it seeks to restrain powerful commercial forces, liberating in its efforts to promote a diversity of choice.

Clive Hollick 1994

120 employees into custody. They had even taken the poor tea boy. If it had been summer they would probably have been ordered to arrest the flies at the newspaper.

Yasar Kemal 1995

♦ The economy is in a terrible state. So what do the people want? Newspapers.

Nilou Mobasser on Iran 2000

♦ Mythomaniac editors know exactly which buttons to push to stimulate outrage. They can then employ a battery of journalistic techniques – repetition, selective reporting, polemic, distortion, hyperbole, factual omission – to ensure that the person or group will be damned for ever more.

Roy Greenslade 2000

♦ The media exists mainly to derive its mission from the government, not to produce a corrective or any dissent. The media, in short, is an extension of the war against Iraq.

Edward Said on the US 2000

♦ In a media regime of personal profiles, instant character assassination, and quasi-information and docusoaps that purport to be true, the past is erased without need for censorship, propaganda and a Ministry of Truth.

Stanley Cohen 2000

♦ Transnational corporations, government propagandists, the mass media and other institutions of coercion and manipulation so distort democracy and liberty that Americans are expected to believe countless lies.

Charles Glass 1996

♦ For all the talk of deregulation, the press is just another business that can no longer ignore either the political realities or its own financial imperatives.

♦ The fact is that the institutional memory of the press about the need for an arm's-length relationship with the government is a fading relic of another era.

James D Squires on the US 1995

♦ The unleashing of market forces in both the press and broadcasting has encouraged some editors and producers to give priority to profits rather than to investigative journalism.

Maurice Frankel 1995

♦ Newspapers are less willing to devote time, space, money and manpower to getting to the bottom of what really happened.

♦ Even worse is the pressure, direct and indirect, from proprietors. It is not, so far as I can tell, that Rupert Murdoch and Conrad Black often intervene to order their papers to take a certain line.

♦ Rupert Murdoch's editors pander to his imagined prejudices, against the monarchy, the BBC and the English upper-middle class.

Godfrey Hodgson 1995

♦ Let me quote a US judge who once said that the horrors with which we are flooded from the tabloid press are just a very small price that we pay for the gift of freedom.

Václav Havel 2002

♦ State censorship in this instance had much less impact than the media's own fixation with maintaining the orthodoxies.

Ronan Bennet on Ireland 2002

♦ The media have abandoned stories. Today they are deemed unreliable because they stem from what we really do and think, from our real experiences, rather than the externally imposed homogenised admass culture allowed us.

Philip Jones Griffiths 1999

♦ The CPJ (Committee to Protect Journalists) said the Russian press played an extremely constructive role during the hostage crisis: 'At a time when the public was apprehensive and afraid, the media provided accurate and timely information about what was happening inside the theatre'. After the raid the press asked questions that the Russian public wanted asked, such as: 'Was every possible measure taken to protect the lives of the hostages?' 'Some of these questions may have made Mr Putin's administration uncomfortable but it is the proper role of the press to take up such issues on behalf of the public'.

Rohan Jayasekera 2003

♦ The broadcast ban on Sinn Fein, the IRA's political allies, backfired so badly that long before John Major decided to scrap it, both Protestants and Catholics in Northern Ireland dismissed the gag as a joke. 'Most people will not be annoyed having this comedy removed from the airwaves,' said Protestant politician Jim Wilson. International broadcasters mocked the British and the ban was made to look simplistic and ineffective as Belfast actors lip-synched the voice of Sinn Fein leader Gerry Adams. Even his cough and laugh were perfectly mimicked.

Michael Grade 1994

♦ It is sadly not uncommon to dismiss as 'outrageous' and 'shocking' and 'dangerous' the powerful presentation of arguments with which people disagree.

Laura Bruni 1995

MEMORY

♦ People come for psychoanalytic treatment because they are remembering in a way that does not free them to forget.

Adam Phillips 2001

♦ Remembering everything is a form of madness.

♦ It is what we need to do with memories, with the images, to make them acceptable and therefore available for consideration – to aestheticise them, to censor them, to eroticise them, to idealise them – that makes the act of memory so fraught. Pieties about the perils of forgetting have made it increasingly difficult to think differently about the purposes of memory; and indeed, about the virtues of forgetting.

Adam Phillips 1999

♦ Without the past, the future would not exist and we would live like animals, ruminating on the present like cows.

Agusto Boal 1999

♦ Continuity needs amnesia. For Japan to have sustained its mobilisation towards economic success, it has had to forget the path taken to reach it.

Jeremy Scott 1995

♦ What is being annihilated with guns, grenades, murders, rape, the displacement of peoples, 'ethnic cleansing', the new ideology supported by the media – is Memory. What is being built on the ruins is the new truth, the one that will one day be the only memory.

Dubravka Ugresic on former Yugoslavia 1994

♦ The Civil Concord Act has not kept its word: Algerians have not spoken out about what happened to them. They are shut away, concealing layers of mute suffering in an ailing collective memory, strictly controlled by those in power.

Daikha Dridi 2001

♦ Even when we are travelling through places that we have left behind, places which have been destroyed or lost, which sound unfamiliar or have names that are new, even then we may suddenly be seized by a memory.

♦ When it comes to recollection, the writer is a past master.

♦ We Germans had the idea of coining a neologism as hackneyed as 'duty of remembrance'.

♦ Attempts to give concrete form to recollection by means of memorials seem doomed to failure.

♦ Experience shows that victims of violence, whoever was responsible for it, do not wish to remember the atrocities they have undergone.

♦ Recently, the Hungarian writer Gyorgy Konrad wrote about Europe: 'To remember is human, we could even say that it is the essence of humanity.'

♦ In recollection, we may speak with both the living and the dead. As long as we are remembered, we live on. Forgetting puts the seal on death.

Günter Grass 2001

♦ There is no cure for memory, though we try to use it to forget with.

Frank Kermode 2001

♦ All over the world, commemorations of atrocities have turned into memory wars.

Stanley Cohen 2001

♦ The ageing individual may argue that the clarity of recollection declines. Societies, however, have usually experienced the reverse.

♦ In Argentina, the youngsters, the children of the 'disappeared' (that word which the military dictators of the 1970s contributed to the language), the eldest aged about 25, the youngest not yet 20, have become the most militant seekers of memory. They call it their 'search for identity'.

Andrew Graham-Yooll 2001

♦ People never spoke about the past; war and the pre-war years have disappeared into a black hole. Every family had its own black hole: the subject was taboo. Too many things in this family have been swept under the carpet.

Birgit on Austria 2000

♦ For three generations, since the Russian Revolution of 1917, Ukrainians were forbidden to remember, let alone speak. As organisations such as Memorial, created to investigate and commemorate the victims of Stalin's repression, began to unearth the mass graves of his victims in Ukraine, oral testimonies emerged to reconstruct a history that had been so long denied.

Judith Vidal-Hall 1999

MIGRATION

♦ British immigration officials have the power to grant or withhold temporary admission at any time without giving reasons for their decision or evidence for their supposition that a detainee 'will not comply with the conditions set', on the grounds that 'we are not a court of law'.

♦ The most common reason for the refusal of asylum is the official denial of political persecution in the refugee's country of origin.

Member of Campaign to Close Campsfield 1994

♦ 'I would put them all on a boat and send them all back to where they came from.'

♦ 'Because, well, we can't look after our own people, can we?'

♦ 'They're scrounging off the country, but not only that. They're doing a lot of shoplifting and everything, aren't they?'

♦ 'No, I haven't seen it. But I've heard about it.'

♦ 'Most of them are here just to see what they can get out of the system. Of the 800 who are listed in Dover, I'd say that only about 50 to 100 are genuine asylum seekers, so they should be allowed to stay, but the others, no.'

Voices from a Dover shopping centre 1998

♦ The Irish suffered media hostility from the nineteenth century on. Even the sainted cartoonist David Low, whose anti-Home Rule credentials were impeccable, caricatured the Irish as simian creatures, confessing that his drawings 'were composed of traditional Irish types of archaic burlesque with button noses, long upper lips and upside-down short cutty pipes. The Jews suffered centuries of prejudice and were routinely referred to in contemptuous terms in the press a century ago. But they became media monsters in the 1930s when they were 'flooding' into Britain and again, after the war, when inaccurately accused of running black market activities in a time when they were killing British soldiers in Palestine. West Indians and Asians from India and Pakistan have been, at various times, cast in the role of monster. Of late, the Roma have suffered a similar fate, along with others from Eastern Europe.

Roy Greenslade 2000

♦ The defensive insulation of a liberal society founded more than ever on conspicuous economic privilege may be as unseemly as the savage wars for geopolitical influence that the West waged during the superpower era. It may even corrupt the thing it is intended to defend, just as the conflicts of the Cold War in Africa, Latin America and Asia corrupted many cherished liberal nostrums in the 'free world' at the time. It was these proxy wars that turned liberalism into a dirty word.

♦ With capital scudding around the world at extraordinary speeds, people may begin to move in larger numbers than they do already.

♦ According to the International Organisation of Migration, there are around 150 million people living outside their country of origin – less than 3% of the world's population. Of these, an even smaller proportion resort to illegal means of entry into other states.

Jeremy Harding 2000

♦ Britain is proud of its reputation as a haven for refugees, it just doesn't want any to come here, that's all.

Jeremy Hardy 1998

♦ Over 80% of the world's refugees, now numbered at close on 50 million, are women and children.

Caroline Moorehead 1998

♦ Amid all the rhetoric over cultural homogeneity and collapsing welfare systems, it's easy to forget that the debate on immigration was once driven by geopolitical considerations. Today, the West's attitude to immigration is insular, expressed as a provincial fear of the outside world.

♦ Immigrants are escaping local, not global, tyranny; the only thing they represent to the West is danger, a threat to cosy post-Cold-War prosperity. 'This asylum business . . . is really just looking for jobs and prosperity in Europe,' says the immigration officer, in disgust. 'There is nothing moral in it, just greed.'

Akash Kapur 2002

♦ In a flash everything I was seeing happening around me in Europe that year – my nationality, my racial identity, my place on this planet and in England, where I could not physically bring myself to say out loud, 'I'm English,' everything made sudden sense, like logical functions in a single all-encompassing formula. It was like stepping into a new skin. For the first time in 33 years I had found a place on earth to stand. I was a migrant. My identity was my very lack of one.

Rohan Jayasekera 2002

♦ Migrants fall into many categories: refugees from persecution, ethnic violence, famine, natural or ecological disaster; searchers for family, friends, sexual freedom, peace, money, work, culture, excitement and many other things.

Bob Sutcliffe 1994

♦ False passports, false identities, erased pasts, uncharted futures, and above all silence. No voice, no representation, no rights, no name. Where poverty and violence are directly linked to a political system how can any distinction between refugees and 'economic migrants' be made?

Irena Maryniak 1997

♦ Their caravans set off; weak, wounded, lonely, defenceless, hopeless. In order to live they must flee, to live they must give up their lands, must go far from their country, their land, their village and leave their graveyard behind. Children cry, not understanding what's going on. The children who know nothing of country, land, migrating, time and fate, do not give up their childhood in this great migration.

Mehmed Uzun 2001

MIGRATE OR DIE
Kamila Shamsie

> 'Everyone has the right to seek and to enjoy
> in other countries asylum from persecution'
> *Universal Declaration of Human Rights Article 14*

'Bogus asylum seekers'. What does the term mean? It means: here are people who want refuge in Britain but (oh, perfidy!) can't prove they were forced to leave their countries in fear for their lives – torture, imprisonment or some equally hideous fate.

It means, quite probably, they're just economic migrants – people who have come to the UK to leech off its social services, take jobs and public housing away from its residents, create massive crowding in its urban centres. And all this while remaining wilfully un-British.

Is it possible to counter these claims by insisting that economic deprivation is itself a form of persecution? That it falls under Article 14 of the UN Declaration of Human Rights? Is it possible to argue that the threat of starvation, of malnourishment, of being forced to send your children to work in factories and farmlands from the age of three, is evidence of the 'cruel and inhumane' treatment of a particular group – the poor and downtrodden of a nation? Can persecution in the passive – indifference, incompetence, venality – be just as insidious and sinister as its more familiar active form? The persecution that is driven by a focused, malignant intent – armed men breaking down your door, for instance.

Yes. And yes again.

If a nation fails to provide its citizens with an existence worthy of human dignity, who can argue with their right to seek it out elsewhere? But of course, the argument against the free movement of economic migrants never explicitly denies people the right to leave their countries of nationality and go elsewhere – the argument merely says let the elsewhere be not-here.

Those who seek to restrict economic migration will doubtless say: 'It's not that we think people should starve, or children be forced to inhale toxic fumes in factories without ventilation; we're just saying it's not our problem. We're just saying, we need to put ourselves first, or we'll be flooded.'

Oh, yes. The flood of refugees. The great onslaught.

What great onslaught?

No one can convincingly argue that Britain today is collapsing under the weight of asylum seekers. All the hysteria is around the projections, the fear of a trend being established that will lead to all sorts of horrors. Well, for every projection there's a counter-projection. For every insistence that London will be overrun with asylum seekers placing unreasonable demands on the city's infrastructure and causing its collapse, others point out that ageing populations and static growth rates, combined with an increase in white-collar workers, means there's a need for economic migration to fill the gaps that are being created.

What, really, is the fear at the heart of the anti-immigrant discourse?

Is it that the entire population of the developing world will arrive in the UK? Unlikely. Asylum-seekers are more likely to go to the nearest place of refuge – because it's cheaper to get there and because it's closer to home in ways that mitigate the process of alienation. While sections of the UK press last year were claiming that the UK had become a haven for asylum-seekers, the country with the greatest refugee crisis was Afghanistan. Only 9,000 came to the UK; over 200,000 went to Pakistan.

As the UK isn't exactly surrounded by nations on the cusp of famine and economic disaster it seems unlikely that it's going to face anything like the problems Pakistan faced through the 1980s and 1990s when the official Afghan refugee numbers crossed the 3 million mark in the space of 15 years – with the United Nations High Commission for Refugees acknowledging that vast numbers of refugees who crossed the porous border were simply never counted. Having lived in Pakistan through this time, I've more than once wondered why it is that I hear so much more about the asylum-seeker crisis in the UK than I ever did in Pakistan – a country far less able than the UK to cope with such a sharp influx of refugees.

And the answer, the simple unmistakable answer, lies in one word which is at the very heart of this asylum argument: race.

The natives are coming. For God's sake, don't let them in.

At university I studied eighteenth- and nineteenth-century imperial texts in which the portrayal of Africans, Asians and Arabs as inferior and in need of civilising bolstered claims to imperial expansion. Today, I can still hear the same language in discussions of asylum-seekers. The difference is that now it's not being used as an incentive to go out and conquer the world, but rather as a reason to erect the barricades and keep the world out.

It's worth mentioning that there is a connection between those days of Empire and the current state of the world. Between 1947 and 1974 as the British pulled out of their colonies, arbitrarily created administrative boundaries became national boundaries, resulting in states with inbuilt instability. This would be problematic in the best of circumstances, but in the post-Empire world of the Cold War it was disastrous. The post-colonial states became pawns for the USSR and the USA, their governments (often undemocratic) bolstered with the economic and military aid they desperately needed precisely because of their inherent instability.

And when the Cold War ended, the superpowers rapidly pulled out, cutting off the aid, leaving nations such as Somalia and Rwanda and Afghanistan to implode.

I don't raise this to evoke imperial guilt, but to assert the need for responsibility and an understanding of how this absurdly imbalanced world of ours got to be the way it is and why all those asylum-seekers are compelled to risk their lives to go to countries that might just be able to restore to them that basic requirement – human dignity.

Where does all this leave us? In a world of consequences. As the past has brought Britain to this present – this complicated present without easy answers but with an absolute need clearly to see and state the problems that exist without hiding behind a smokescreen of racist imagery and apocalyptic predictions – so the choices Britain makes now will define the arguments of the next decades. The most crucial choice that seems to be facing the Western world at this point is whether or not to let fear govern decisions.

● Should fear of the outsider, of the possible-terrorist, of foreign leeches govern this nation's choices as it defines itself in a rapidly changing world?

● Is it better to turn away 1,000 people who only want security and who will work for it, than risk letting in one whose purpose in coming here is altogether more nefarious?

● Is it better to cling to already outdated ideas of who you are and what you look like than to accept that there is a need to re-define what it means to be British in the twenty first century?

There is much that needs to be worked out in the migration debate – but it must start with this belief: if you lock the doors, you only lock yourself in.

MINORITIES

♦ Minorities and others who have lacked political power are always disadvantaged by curbs on speech and expression, and a largely untold story is how they have been targeted in current debate over hate speech: all censorship laws and trends have been used to silence the voices of blacks and other minorities.

♦ In 1976, for example, the board of the Island Trees school district on Long Island removed nine books from the school library on the grounds that they were 'un-American, anti-Christian, and just plain filthy'. Little noted at the time or since was the fact that seven of the nine were by minority authors, including *Black Boy* by Richard Wright, *A Hero Ain't Nothing but a Sandwich* by Alice Childress and works by Langston Hughes and Piri Thomas.

Gara La Marche on the US 1995

♦ On 13 May, the day that Czech President Václav Havel paid tribute to Romani victims of Nazi genocide during the *Porajmos* (Gypsy Holocaust), a Czech Roma man was brutally murdered in a racist attack on his home. That same weekend Ion Cioaba, the Romanian 'King of Romanies Everywhere', declared: 'The Romani lived far better under Ceaucescu. They had jobs and were able to raise children. Now they can hardly make ends meet.'

Vitaly Shentalinsky 1991

♦ There is no reason at all for this inhuman, purposeless war in Anatolia. The Kurds want nothing but human rights. They want to use their language, to have their identity restored, and develop their culture to the same extent as the Turkish people. You will ask if the Turkish people have these rights themselves. If things continue as they are, it will not be long before we encounter waves of resistance for the Turkish people. These 70 years have crushed all the people of Anatolia like a steamroller; not a blade of grass has grown in its path. For the moment, all we can ask is that all the Anatolian people be granted full human rights.

Yasar Kemal 1995

♦ Before 1948, the Jewish community in Palestine owned a little over 6% of the land. Now only Jewish citizens have access to that land.

Edward Said 1998

♦ While Oskar Schindler choked on the smoke of burning flesh at Plaszow, and the Auschwitz furnaces blackened the sky, Stalin was taking a lunatic's revenge on his own people. Some Nazi camps were simply taken over, the same barbed wire used to imprison ordinary Soviet citizens on 'liberated' territory. As part of this process, entire nationalities were deported from Soviet Europe to Central Asia.

♦ On the night of 18 May 1944, Tatars in the Crimea were woken and given 10 minutes to leave their homes. More than 180,000 people, jammed into goods wagons, were subjected to a suffocating 20-day journey to Uzbekistan.

♦ The Soviet model for persecution on grounds of nationality had been set in 1937, with the exile of ethnic Koreans from the Soviet Far East, on grounds of 'spying for Japan'. Ethnic Finns from the Leningrad area followed them in 1942.

♦ Having dealt with the Tatars, secret police chief Lavrenty Beria offered to deport Crimea's Armenian, Bulgarian and Greek population as well. The standard pretext for deportation was alleged collaboration with the German occupying army. The Crimean Greeks, accused of 'reviving private trade', were an exception. Given their bitter experience of Stalinism, the scale of Tatar collaboration was smaller than might have been expected. When the news of their deportation was made public two years later, it was implicitly recognised that active collaborators were in a minority. The many were blamed for failing to prevent the anti-Soviet activities of the few – an accusation that could equally well have been levelled against the peninsula's majority population of Russians and Ukrainians.

Stephen Mulvey 1994

♦ For the approximately four million Romani living in eastern Europe, the fall of Communism has had both negative and positive consequences. On the positive side, there is greater freedom to travel, to set up organisations – including political parties – and to publish their own newspapers and magazines. On the negative side, racist propaganda is flourishing and racist violence is tolerated.

Donald Kenrick 1994

♦ Our country's chilly attitude towards all strangers, bears particularly heavily on the Roma. Even though they are German citizens, the Sinti who have lived here for several generations feel themselves despised and isolated. The Roma exist without any protection or support; nor is there any state that will come to their aid.

♦ These 'travelling people' have difficulty finding anywhere to stay. We even find other foreigners, themselves barely tolerated among us, expressing their own intolerance the moment the Gypsies appear on the horizon.

♦ Those we call the Gypsies are a long way ahead of us in at least one respect: they are the natural inhabitants of a 'Europe without frontiers'.

Günter Grass 1998

MULTICULTURALISM

♦ Inter-cultural understanding isn't an idyllic state that happens naturally; it's hard work.

Wolfgang Thierse 2001

♦ It's no good pretending a multicultural society can be held together by a pact of mutual indifference between ethnic communities living separately from each other in a set of intellectual and spiritual bell jars.

Michael Ignatieff 2002

♦ Whereas racial theorists used to say that social differences were the inevitable product of natural differences and there was nothing we could do about it, multiculturalists argue that they are the product of cultural differences and there is nothing we should do about it. But this is simply to rename inequality.

Kenan Malik 1997

♦ Race has been a perennial source of discord in science for the past half century, despite the widespread Western belief that it has been conclusively discredited as a theme of scientific knowledge.

Marek Kohn 1999

♦ 'I say I'm black. Sylvia is black. Kathy and Anne, we are from the same island – but we have the family tree and our family history a long way back. But someone here in England wants to tell me that I am from Africa. But I say what part of Africa? It's nonsense. My great-great-grandfather was a Welshman – should I hold on to that, too? I'm not Afro-Caribbean, either. I hate to be classified like that.'

Diane 1995

♦ Throughout history all cultures have fed one another, been grafted onto one another and, in the process, our world has been enriched. The disappearance of a culture is the loss of a colour, a different light, a different source.

Yasar Kemal on the Kurds of Turkey 1995

MUSIC

♦ In 1942 the BBC published the following four-point statement of policy with regard to certain types of music and performances:

1. To exclude any form of anaemic or debilitated vocal performance by male singers.

2. To exclude any insincere and over-sentimental style of performance by women singers.

3. To exclude numbers which are slushy in sentiment or contain innuendo or other matter considered to be offensive from the point of view of good taste and of religious or Allied susceptibilities.

4. To exclude numbers, with or without lyrics, which are based on tunes from standard classical works.

I am sure that the BBC's policy statement of 1942 has long been superseded: indeed, it might even appear comic nowadays. But point 3 will continue to apply. It can be regarded as part and parcel of the censorship that can be found in all periods and cultures.

♦ Music has always been affected by the needs of religious and political propaganda. The reforms brought in by the Council of Trent in the sixteenth century were deliberately designed to ensure that in performances of church music the religious music was right in the forefront. The motives underlying such reforms and the methods for putting them into effect were hardly dissimilar from those of Zhdanov and others in Soviet Russia trying to use music to support an optimistic socialist ideology.

♦ Music continues to be approved or disapproved according to its impact on particular cultural or religious sensibilities. Beethoven's fate in Maoist and post-Maoist China is a ludicrous story. In Israel there is a continual debate as to whether the music of Wagner and Strauss should be played in public concerts and broadcast on the radio. At present both composers are, to my knowledge, banned – though presumably recordings of them, playable in the home, are not. At one stage it was apparently impossible for my own oratorio, *A Child of Our Time*, to be performed in Israel because it contained the name *Jesus*. That, I'm glad to say, no longer applies.

♦ Censorship exists, then, in all societies, be they communist, fascist, democratic or whatever. In its worst manifestations, it is part of a complex of restraints on personal liberty. Discovering the whole truth about it entails de-schooling society, not just expressing abhorrence or condemning those on the opposite side from ourselves. For my part, I can only salute those who manage to break through: people like Shostakovich who, in his music, often used officially acceptable 'programmes' as a kind of 'front' or alibi, whilst communicating to the world – inside and outside Russia – both the distress and the courage of countless individuals; people like Nadezhda Mandelstam who memorised all her husband's poetry to keep it alive. From such people we constantly get signals, which tell us that the individual has somehow the fortitude to survive.

♦ I received one such signal when I read a line by a young Polish poet, Jacek Bierezin, whose censored work was published in *Index on Censorship* 2/1975. It said, 'Cherish men but do not choose nations.' I am sure that a lot of censored music, all over the world, would say just that, if it were allowed to be performed.

Michael Tippett 1983

♦ There are of course certain types of real music which are censored – and this is in itself a token of its power. This has been recognised by governments and philosophers since the time of Plato. Music in some regimes has charms only when it conforms to the propaganda of the day; in these regimes it not art but power which is music to the ears. I remember in Russia in 1945 hearing an oratorio, for that is what it was, in praise of Lenin. Again, in China, until recently, music and musicians suffered considerably under the Gang of Four.

♦ Commercial interests and tyrants: both attempt the censorship of music, the former by harnessing its potency for financial gain, the latter for the consolidation of their power.

Yehudi Menuhin 1983

♦ Shostakovitch's success presented the Soviets with a problem: he had become a much-sought-after cultural phenomenon abroad. The foreign press wrote about him and this was worrying. Remember, during

this whole period the three most famous living Russian composers – Profokiev, Stravinsky and Rachmaninov – are all living abroad. Now, suddenly, here was a boy already famous in the West and, understandably, there was an urge to say, Look what our Soviet cultural system can produce: it produces geniuses. 'You in the West no longer have Beethovens, only decadents like Schoenberg and Stravinsky. Here we have Shostakovitch.' But there's a worry because it's clear this art is difficult, not 'proletarian'.

Gerard McBurney 1998

♦ The most thorough-going and systematic attacks on music this century have been in the Soviet Union between 1932 and 1953, and in the Third Reich.

♦ It would be comforting to think that music censorship didn't take place in democratic societies. Comforting but, unfortunately, quite wrong.

♦ The BBC may have given up patrolling the parameters of popular musical tastes, but the years since are none the less littered with examples of banned and marginalised records which suggest that, for the Corporation, music is still a potentially subversive force.

♦ Music has power. As a means of communicating dissent it has few competitors, and it binds as tightly as any other cultural ties. Little wonder then, that music so often draws the censors' fire, even if their assaults eventually prove futile. As the Exodus dub has it: 'Babylon them try to ban the beat / but Jah say Exodus we have to / Beat the ban.'

Julien Petley 1998

♦ The Nazis planned to use music, as well as other arts, as a political tool to unify and educate the racially pure German Volk. The music they banned was enormously varied, as were the lives of the composers. Racial considerations aside, what it had in common were either elements of jazz or atonal music. German composers who were experimenting with new musical forms were also targeted. This music was presented as symptomatic of a cancer infecting German culture. The Nazi propaganda ministry wanted to educate the public about its danger and to revitalise the concept of a pure German music as exemplified by Wagner and Bruckner. Ironically, many people attended the 1938 *Entartete Musik* (Degenerate Music) exhibition in the hope of hearing Kurt Weill, one of the 'degenerate' composers.

♦ The *Entartete* programme became a policy of censorship that supported the ethnic and political cleansing of German society. Many exceptionally gifted artists were imprisoned and eventually murdered.

♦ A number of these artists were among the western European Jewish intelligentsia sent to the Theresienstadt (Terezín) concentration camp just north of Prague.

♦ Remarkably, despite the horror of the living conditions inside the camp, by a variety of ingenious means musical instruments were smuggled into Terezín as early as the second transport. At first, concerts were held secretly in attics and basements of the barracks. The performances increased with the growing number of amateur and professional artists arriving with each transport. Upon discovery of the secret performances, the Nazis realised the importance of culture to the lives of the prisoners in Theresienstadt and initially permitted such cultural activities. They would manipulate these activities as the tide of war changed, using them for propaganda purposes to counter evidence and reports of 'atrocities' filtering to the Allies.

Mark Ludwig 1998

♦ Before releasing Christopher Wallace (The Notorious BIG)'s *Ready to Die* album, Sean 'Puff Daddy' Combs demanded that Wallace exercise a little self-censorship on 'Gimme the Loot' to avoid repercussions that might damage the commercial chances of his new artist. 'Gimme the Loot' is a dialogue between two burglars, a duo so desperate for survival that robbing a pregnant woman is no longer a reprehensible act: 'I don't give a fuck if you're pregnant / Give me the baby rings and the "number one mom" pendant.' Wallace refused to change his verse and the album, complete with violence and lewd sexual language, got past the media

UN SALUDO AFECTUOSO EN LOS PRIMEROS
100 NÚMEROS DE "INDEX ON CENSORSHIP"

PLOMO
MEX-ABRIL 88

scrutiny of C Delores Tucker (a former civil rights activist who lobbied for the banning of certain rap records) and the censorship watchdogs via a strange garble on the disc at the strategic moment.

Miles Marshall Lewis 1998

♦ There is so much I could do for my country if only they would give me my 'musical freedom' without 'cutting me down to size', without 'tripping me up', ruining my plans, without trying to destroy me as a person and as a musician, just to prove that a talented personality can be broken too if he misbehaves, and that a mediocrity can be put in his place.

Mstislav Rostropovich on Russia 1998

♦ On 12 January 1991, the day before the United Nations deadline for Saddam Hussein's compliance with its resolution demanding the Iraqi withdrawal from Kuwait ran out, Giles Peterson, a DJ and director of the commercial radio station Jazz FM, played 90 minutes of 'peace music' to show his opposition to war. He also broadcast details of peace marches that were taking place in London that afternoon. As a result, he was sacked.

Martin Cloonan 1998

MUSIC: SOUNDS OF HATE?
Martin Cloonan

Music is perhaps the purest of all art forms. Its power to
express emotion, to describe the human condition, to
change moods and to fulfil lives makes it unique. It is also
intensely democratic. Art and literature may reveal their
secrets only to those in the know, music is accessible to all.
It is perhaps because of its ubiquity and accessibility that
music has often frightened the powerful who have sought to
control it, limit its scope and in extreme cases – such as that
of the Taliban regime in Afghanistan – to ban it entirely.

The power of music to disturb the equilibrium within society has long been recognised. Writing some four hundred
years before the birth of Christ, Plato argued that the power
of music was that: 'By gradual infiltration it softly overflows
upon the characteristic pursuits of men and from those
issues forth grown greater to attack their business dealings,
and from these relations it proceeds against the laws and
constitution with wanton licence till it finally overthrows
all things public and private.'

Some rulers took this message to heart and, down the ages,
the authorities have sought to control music, as the following examples show. In the twelfth century, Welsh harp
music became subject to official regulation. In the seven-

teenth century, Oliver Cromwell suppressed the use of choirs and organs in churches and John Gay's *Polly*, his follow-up to *The Beggar's Opera*, was suppressed by the Lord Chamberlain. In the nineteenth century, Denmark's colonisation of Greenland included the suppression of traditional Eskimo drums and, by the nineteenth century, music hall in the UK was also fighting – and sometimes losing – censorial battles.

The twentieth century's two most dictatorial regimes – Nazi Germany and the USSR – both sought to control music. Interestingly, both used the language of moral decay to decry music of which they disapproved. In Hitler's Germany in 1938, an exhibition of *Entartete Musik* (degenerate music), highlighting the alleged depravity of Jewish and black jazz musicians, toured the country in an attempt to keep the *volk* pure. In the Soviet Union during the 1930s jazz was attacked; in the 1950s and '60s it was rock, often denounced as a sign of decadent capitalist values.

Meanwhile, the century's most racist dictatorship, apartheid South Africa, also sought to censor music, especially that which mixed the races or criticised the ruling National Party regime.

But dictatorships were not the only censors. Despite having a constitution that guarantees freedom of speech, the USA has witnessed a range of attacks on music. Over the years, for instance, numerous church leaders, especially in the Bible Belt of the southern states, have campaigned against forms of 'the Devil's music'. Particular targets have been blues and rock'n'roll which were alleged to have originated in voodoo rituals. A more sophisticated campaign was waged in the 1980s by the Parents' Music Resource Center (PMRC). This was successful in getting warning stickers placed on albums and in general spreading a chill factor throughout the music industry.

In Britain, attacks on popular music have often been led by the press. In September 1956, the *Daily Mail* warned its readers about the perils of rock'n'roll: 'It is deplorable. It is tribal. And it is from America. It follows ragtime, blues, dixie, jazz, hot cha cha and boogie woogie, which surely originated in the jungle. We sometimes wonder whether it is the negroes' revenge.'

In the 1960s, the *News of The World* led an attack on pop that culminated in the arrest of Rolling Stones Mick Jagger and Keith Richards. In the 1970s, the press was heavily implicated in the sacking of the Sex Pistols by EMI – this time the *Mail* wrote of 'the mercenary manipulation of pop' – and in the moves against raves in the 1980s when the *Sun* headlined with 'Shoot these evil acid bastards'. In 1994, the *Daily Star* welcomed the rapper Snoop Doggy Dogg to the UK with the front-page headline: 'Kick This Evil Bastard Out'; in 2001, the *Daily Express* headlined its front page with 'Get Out' when Eminem toured.

There has also been a history of various pressure groups campaigning against popular music. In the UK the most famous of these, the National Viewers' and Listeners' Association (NVALA – now known as Media Watch UK), was founded in 1965. It has campaigned against a range of popular musicians including the Rolling Stones, Alice Cooper, Chuck Berry and the Sex Pistols, occasionally drumming up support from MPs.

In recent years, perhaps the most censored scene in the UK has been that of neo-Nazi bands. But in contrast to Germany, which has a much bigger neo-Nazi rock scene and where there has been a much more overt state-led clampdown, the British government has not openly intervened in this scene.

Perhaps the most interesting development in recent years has come from elements of the liberal Left whose promotion of 'political correctness' has had obvious implications for freedom of expression. One arena where political correctness has been particularly apparent is that of gay rights, and most attention in this area has centred on the white rapper Eminem. In May 2000, Gay and Lesbian Alliance (GLAAD) of the USA attacked his album *The Marshall Mathers LP* for being homophobic, and called upon him to be more 'responsible' in his lyrics. In January 2001, GLAAD and the UK-based Outrage! condemned Elton John for appearing with Eminem at the Grammy awards in Los Angeles where the album was to be nominated as 'album of the year'. When the event went ahead (complete with the duet), it was picketed by gay activists. These were countered by others, including a group calling themselves Faggots for Eminem.

In the following month, the Students Union at Sheffield University banned Eminem records from its radio station and bars, within which the wearing of Eminem T-shirts was also banned. Reviews of Eminem in the student newspaper were also vetoed in a move the Union said was aimed at creating a culture of respect for all. The same month the rapper's shows at Manchester Arena were picketed by student union gay organisations and Outrage! The latter also called for the Ministry of Sound Club in London to cancel a proposed Eminem performance.

In August 2002, the BBC removed the track 'Log on' by the reggae artist Elephant Man from a website it had set up to accompany the BBC2 television series *The History of Reggae* because the song describes stamping on and setting fire to a gay man. Another track, 'Bun di Chi Chi' (burn the queer), was also removed. In October, Outrage! picketed the Music of Black Origin (MOBO) awards in London to protest at the inclusion of Elephant Man, Capelton and TOK in the list of nominations, as all three were accused of inciting homophobia. In December, Peter Tatchell of Outrage! called for musicians whose music advocated attacking gays to be prosecuted under the Public Order Act of 1986.

Censors have rarely recognised the complexity of music. Parody is frequently taken at face value and subtleties ignored. Above all, would-be censors have tended to assume that singers are routinely working in the first person in a way that is not so often assumed in film and literature. Thus a complex form is simplified in order to justify censorship. But for as long as music can provoke hate, as well as inspire love, attempts to censor seem destined to continue.

See also www.freemuse.org

NATIONALISM
NUCLEAR POWER

NATIONALISM

♦ 'Everyone has the right to a nationality.'

Universal Declaration of Human Rights Article 15

♦ After 1948, Israeli policy towards the Palestinians clearly envisioned that community's disappearance or its political nullity.

Edward Said 1998

♦ If we are too careful, slow, hesitant and reserved, the new order could be built by others, in particular the nationalists and chauvinists.

Václav Havel on Eastern Europe 1997

♦ Nationalism is that 'revolt against history' which seeks to close what cannot any longer be closed. To fence in what should be frontierless.

Salman Rushdie 1997

♦ When you translate from the language of communism into the language of democracy, you need to change both the *vocabulary* and the *grammar*.

♦ If you want to translate from the language of communism into the language of nationalism, all you need to change is the vocabulary. The grammar remains the same. The type of mental structures that the new system builds up are based on the foundations that already existed under communism. It is us versus them, it is inclusion versus exclusion, and violence as a legitimate way of achieving previously ideological, and now national, goals.

Konstanty Gebert 1999

♦ 'The Border' is part of the lexicon of Irish politics, even for those who have never crossed it. The Border – it's as if we have ceased to think of it as an international line on a map, even though it is an international frontier. and although it follows a few appropriate burrens and drumlin tops and an occassional river, the Irish Border is a strange old line, like the Bosnian-Croatian frontier and the boundaries of most Middle Eastern nations.

Robert Fisk 1998

NUCLEAR POWER

♦ Within Israel, a combination of tight military censorship and self-censorship ensures there is no discussion of nuclear matters; Israel's secret services strangled any potential debate in parliament by threatening members of the Knesset and scientists seeking to testify.

Meir Vanunu 1991

♦ You have to know that no matter what happens, I am proud of my actions, for my revelations, for not cooperating with their lies, for not keeping silent. That is all that a man can do, to not be afraid of the power of the state; to show to all that in the nuclear age a man is obliged to all the human race.

Mordechai Vanunu on Israel's nuclear capability 1991

♦ For those unaffected, memory of disaster is short. Who, in the well-heeled West, now recalls that the world first learned of the Chernobyl accident from Swedish scientists and American spy satellites? Or that Gorbachev, promoter of *glasnost*, was, like the world beyond Soviet borders, kept in the dark about the enormity of the accident and the irradiation problems his country faced; or that the period of panic when fallout rained down on western Europe was accompanied by confusion and disinformation, that scientific reports from affected areas were fragmentary, filtered, impossible to validate?

♦ Russia, a nuclear state whose other Chernobyl-type reactors are still essential to power supplies, had a powerful political need to bury the Chernobyl image as quickly as possible. Worldwide cynicism and distrust were inevitable. But the real tragedy of Chernobyl is not that its immediate consequences and immense long-term problems are fading

from memory, minimised, played down, obfuscated by the governments and protection agencies of the former Soviet Union and the western world, but that as a disaster it is still growing and that in many ways it is far worse than anyone predicted.

♦ At this time, little science of Western standard was emerging from the affected areas. Worse, the highly prestigious scientific journal *Nature* had been accused of censoring Chernobyl fallout information by accepting papers from western groups and then failing to publish them, and Britain's National Radiological Protection Board stood accused of failing to correct misleading undermeasurement of fallout over Britain, published in its first scientific report. Transfer of the essential science and skills in pathology and epidemiology, crucial to the future of large and suffering populations, was being blocked. This was not cock-up: it was cover-up.

♦ Nuclear states, trapped in the same schizophrenic dilemma whatever their colour, sought future safety in all honesty. Yet they also hoped that Chernobyl could be buried in blurred statistics and contradictory arguments, from which its legacy could never be convincingly unravelled.

♦ The US government had, and still has, powerful political reasons for obfuscating these findings. Its Department of Defence is inundated by civil compensation actions from US citizens seeking damages for thyroid cancer and other health detriments, claimed to result from exposure to radio-iodine and other fallout around the Hanford reactors and from weapons test sites in Nevada and elsewhere.

♦ One disgrace is that the world's discredited radiation protection community remained and remains silent. Fortunately, on a narrow front, truth is winning.

Anthony Tucker 1996

♦ But in our place, they brought me in a twig from the yard, and I observed that it was emitting radiation . . . the gamma-spectrometer shower Iodine-131 and other 'young' radionuclides . . . Later we tested soil and trees from many regions of Belarus, and the Institute started to measure the specific activity of foodstuffs arriving for the Institute canteen and crèche.

♦ We started to ring our relatives and friends in Minsk, advising them about safety measures. But this did not last long: at around midday, our telephones were cut off. And a couple of days later we specialists were celled into the Secrecy Department, and made to sign a 29-point document forbidding us to divulge secrets connected with the accident at the Chernobyl plant. These included the structure of the RDMK-1000 reactor, the amount of uranium, etc, 'secrets' that had already been published in scientific literature.

♦ We went home from work without looking from side to side; it was painful to see how the children were playing in the radioactive sand and eating ices.

♦ In our street, I went up to a street vendor and told her to stop selling her sausages, as radioactive rain was falling. But she just said: 'Be off, you drunkard! If there'd been an accident, they'd have announced it on radio and TV.' A naive soul, she believed in the righteousness of the Soviet authorities.

Mikhail Byckau, a Chernobyl assessor, 1996

♦ Russia still has 27,000 nuclear warheads. The West can ensure they do not fall into the wrong hands.

David Hearst 1996

♦ A secret 1995 study of the Strategic Command, *Essentials of Post-Cold War Deterrence*, released through the Freedom of Information Act, advocates that the US exploits its nuclear arsenal to portray itself as 'irrational and vindictive if its vital interests are attacked'.

Noam Chomsky on the US 2000

♦ On 2 February, shattering decades of silence on Tel Aviv's 'nuclear ambiguity', a highly taboo subject, Knesset Member Issam Mahoul initiated the Israeli parliament's first ever debate on Israel's nuclear arsenal. It followed the release in November of 1,200 pages of heavily edited testimony from Mordechai Vanunu, the Israeli nuclear technician who was jailed for 18 years in 1986 for revealing Israel's nuclear secrets to the *Sunday Times*. Mahoul has also called for the release of Mordechai Vanunu, whom he regards as a 'prisoner of conscience, a prisoner of peace, of the struggle for peace'.

Tony Geraghty 2000

O

OBSCENITY

ORGANISATIONS

OWNERSHIP

OBSCENITY

♦ A book, a pamphlet, paper, writing, drawing, painting, representation, figure or any other object, shall be deemed to be obscene if it is lascivious or appeals to the prurient interest or if its effect, or (where it comprises two or more distinct items) the effect of any one of its items is, if taken as a whole, such as to tend to deprave and corrupt persons who are likely, having regard to all relevant circumstances, to read, see or hear the matter contained or embodied in it.

Indian Penal Code section 292

♦ Sin, as Pascal reminds us, is geographical and the same is the case with obscenity.

Soli J Sorabjee *Censorship: A World Encyclopaedia*

♦ Controls on sexually explicit material in Western societies have traditionally been expressed in terms of indecency or obscenity, which are essentially moral concepts. The terms, in particular 'obscene', might be variously defined (or in some cases left undefined, such as under English customs and post office legislation), as a tendency to deprave and corrupt: 'English obscene publications Act 1959'.

Colin Manchester *Censorship: A World Encyclopaedia*

♦ It has long been a principle of adult obscenity law that no matter how shocking or how offensive a sexually explicit work might otherwise be, it is protected speech if it demonstrates serious artistic value.

♦ Anxiety over sexual expression has reached such heights that the president has just signed into law the Communications Decency Act, a measure that will criminalise not just obscenity but even profane language when publicly transmitted in cyberspace.

Amy Adler on the US 1996

♦ An article shall be deemed to be obscene if its effect or (where the article comprises two or more distinct items) the effect of any one of its items is, if taken as a whole, such as to tend to deprave and corrupt persons who are likely, having regard to all relevant circumstances, to read, see or hear the matter contained or embodied in it.

Obscene Publications Act UK 1959

♦ Under the various Censorship of Publications Acts 1929 to 1967 the Ministry of Justice, through the Censorship of Publications Board, has the power to ban the imprint and distribution of books, as well as other publications. The two categories for banning are indecency or obscenity, and information advocating contraception or abortion.

Lynne Walsh on Ireland 1996

ORGANISATIONS

♦ Among the key free speech organisations in the West are the following. The IFEX website gathers together these and many of the growing number of similar organisations in countries throughout Asia, Africa, Latin America and the former Soviet bloc.

Amnesty An international non-governmental human rights organisation with over a million members and offices in more than 55 countries. Through appeals to governments, reports and publicity events, it campaigns for the rights of all those persecuted for their beliefs, origins, gender, sexuality or economic status. It was awarded the Nobel Peace prize in 1977. www.amnesty.org

Article 19, the International Centre Against Censorship, works impartially and systematically to identify and oppose censorship worldwide, through research, publications and campaigning. www.article19.org

Committee to Protect Journalists (CPJ), founded in New York in 1981, is an international non-governmental organisation that aims to enable journalists around the world to continue with their work unmolested, by publicising cases of persecution and giving practical support to those under legal and physical threat. www.cpj.org

Human Rights Watch (HRW), through reports and campaigns, advocates for legislation that protects and enhances expression rights, and protests against government actions and policies and court decisions that stifle open discussion. www.hrw.org

IFEX (International Free Expression Exchange), founded in Toronto in 1993, exists to help co-ordinate the activities of the world's freedom of expression organisations and to facilitate communication between them. It provides a database of freedom of expression violations, bringing together the reports of various organisations, and carrying 'action alerts' to promote concerted action. Its website carries links to its growing number of members worldwide. canada.ifex.org

Index (Index on Censorship), founded in 1972, is the only magazine devoted to protecting and promoting free expression. International in outlook, publishing some of the world's finest writers, *Index* exposes the stories *they* didn't want you to know, engages in controversial debates on the limits of free speech and gives the background behind the world headlines. In its 30-year history it has become a haven for silenced journalists, artists, writers, film-makers and musicians. Each issue includes a name-by-name monitor of the censored throughout the world. www.indexonline.org

International Federation of Journalists (IFJ) promotes international action to defend press freedom and social justice through strong, free and independent trade unions of journalists. It supports journalists and their unions whenever they are fighting for their industrial and professional rights and has established an International Safety Fund to provide humanitarian aid for journalists in need. www.ifj.org

International PEN was founded in London in 1921 as a club for poets, essayists, editors and novelists. In response to political events, it quickly became one of the first organisations to work for human rights. It promotes writers' rights in all areas, from the translation and defence of minority literatures to campaigning for the release of imprisoned writers. www.oneworld.org/internatpen

Reporters Sans Frontières, recognised by the French government as an organisation in the public interest, offers material and legal assistance to imprisoned and persecuted journalists around the world, as well as working to encourage debate on problems connected with press freedom. www.rsf.org

OWNERSHIP

♦ Monopoly is a terrible thing, until you have it.

Rupert Murdoch 1994

♦ Is the consumption of ideas and images really no different from the consumption of goods? The ideas and images that the mass media disseminate shape collective life, for social values and determine the course of history. The information that individuals absorb becomes part of the culture that everyone shares in ways that have different consequences than choices in toothpaste or breakfast cereal.

♦ How few owners, controlling what percentage of a nation's mass communications, constitute a menace to democracy?

Leo Bogart 1994

♦ There was a time when US newspaper owners and journalists alike – the world's most unrestrained guardians of free expression – wallowed in the shallow protection afforded their craft by the First Amendment to the US Constitution. And whenever threatened, they wrapped themselves in a fragile armour made from a couple of narrow twentieth-century Supreme Court rulings prohibiting government restraint.

♦ But after a 25-year evolution that has changed both the culture of the press and the nature of its ownership, the fear and the threat of government censorship has subsided. There is universal agreement among press leaders and legal experts that the technological explosion in communications has made government suppression of free speech impossible.

♦ So now, in quest of survival and prosperity in the twenty-first century world of internets and information superhighways, the owners of the US press are marching carelessly in lockstep down a course of self-censorship that makes government taming needless, but infinitely easier none the less.

James D Squires 1995

♦ A free and diverse media are an indispensable part of the democratic process. They provide a multiplicity of voices and opinions that inform the public, influence opinion and engender political debate. They promote the culture of dissent which any healthy democracy must have.

In so doing they contribute to the cultural fabric of the nation and help define our sense of identity and purpose. If one voice becomes too powerful, this process is placed in jeopardy and democracy is damaged. Special media ownership rules, which exist in all major markets, are needed therefore to provide the safeguards necessary to maintain diversity and plurality.

UK Government White Paper May 1995

♦ Virtually all the free and identifiable broadcast news gathering in the world, save the British government-supported BBC, is now controlled by companies for which journalism is a mere sideline to more important and infinitely more profitable businesses. True, there is little chance of all the big communications czars conspiring to slant or censor the news. But the chances of the news media ever being able to report accurately, completely and with credibility on themselves or, for that matter, each other, are no better.

James D Squires 1995

♦ Those with the gold rule – and for the most part own – the means of communication. What we get to think and know about the world is firmly in the hands of a few.

Philip Jones Griffiths 1999

♦ When a war-weary Colombian listens to a news story on the radio or television he or she is drawn into another battle: the information battle. This battle is fought not by journalists, but by the two most powerful economic groups in the country – the Santodomingo Group and the Ardila Lulle Group.

♦ Media ownership is highly concentrated. Five out of every 10 news stories are generated by the Santodomingo group, four out of 10 by the Ardila Lulle Group. Only one out of 10 stories is from any other source.

♦ Santodomingo and Ardila Lulle are not just media conglomerates. Their interests include manufacturing, banking and commerce and their radio and television stations carry the bulk of their companies' advertising. Money thus circulates within the corporations. Now that the two groups have signed an agreement that lets them advertise on each other's television stations, money also circulates between them.

♦ Faced with this concentration of ownership, most journalists opt for self-censorship. Journalists invoke the old adage: the goal of journalism is to make friends, not enemies.

Fabio Castillo on Colombia 2000

♦ One of the problems of free expression in the US press is the high concentration of ownership in the media world.

Freimut Duve 2002

PATRIOTISM

PHOTOGRAPHY

POLITICAL CORRECTNESS

PORNOGRAPHY

POVERTY

PRISON

PRIVACY

PROPAGANDA

PATRIOTISM

♦ Patriotism is the stated reason for what is at the same time the most menacing and the most frivolous attack on the American tradition of openness. That is a proposed constitutional amendment to allow criminal punishment of anyone who desecrates the American flag.

Anthony Lewis 1995

♦ Turkish governments have resolved to drain the pool to catch the fish; to declare all-out war on the Kurds. We have already seen how it can be done. The world is also aware of it. Only the people of Turkey have been kept in ignorance; newspapers have been forbidden to write about the drainage. Or maybe there was no need for censorship: maybe our press, with its sense of patriotism and strong nationalist sentiment, chose not to write about it assuming the world would neither hear nor see what was happening. The water was being drained in so horrendous a fashion that the smoke ascended to high heaven. But for our press, deceiving the world and our people – or, rather, believing they had succeeded in doing so – was the greatest act of patriotism, of nationalism. They were not aware that they had perpetrated a crime against humanity.

Yasar Kemal 1995

♦ As for the very notion of patriotism, it falters before the perfectly obvious interdependence of the nations, as well as the universal prospect of mass obliteration by the atom bomb, the instrument which has doomed us, so to speak, to this lengthy peace between the great powers.

Arthur Miller 1978

♦ Violent nationalism which at all times in history has wrapped itself in the mantle of patriotism claiming to act 'for the good of the 'nation.' And always, too, leaves behind nothing but ruins, destruction, blood and tears.

Yacov Guterman 2000

♦ Our writer knows that the war has changed everything: no one is the same any more; even his own reality, his own norms, have vanished. In their place a new reality is coming into being before his eyes: new values are being established, a new world is being built into which life will be breathed once it is named.

♦ An alarm bell rings in our writer's head: his work, that of a writer, is not, and cannot be, adherence to one truth. But in the new relationship between his and his audience, there is room for only ONE truth – or what has been proclaimed as the truth. Everything else is a lie.

♦ Our writer finds himself in a new communicative situation akin to that of the photographic, in which, like a double exposure, things overlap even within himself: he no longer knows where the private person ends and the writer begins, where the boundaries between his heart and his mind lie. In this fragmented state, he is being asked to provide something he does not understand and that is beyond his strength: he is being asked to be the spokesman of his people, the loudspeakers and conveyor of 'correct' political truths, a soothsayer and a leader, a popular singer and a healer, examiner of the 'national being' and its spiritual renovator.

♦ In the newly-established and paranoid communications order, in their everyday life, his colleagues are suddenly waging invisible wars for the right way, the right idea. They are suddenly surrounded by a self-styled army of little patriot-informers who slip them reports about the antipatriotic behaviour of this or that colleague. What is at stake is what is right, what is at stake are the sincere patriotic feelings and all methods are permissible. Forget methods: this is being done in the name of the homeland, which is in danger. Without noticing it, his colleagues are slowly becoming policemen, courtiers who take the collective patriotic pulse.

♦ From the history of my people, this writer's people, I have learned what misfortunes result from confusing roles: for the writers themselves, for their people, for the freedom of speech, for literature itself.

Therefore, as a writer I shall not defend the barricades of my homeland. I prefer to stroll along the barricade of literature or sit awhile on the barricade of freedom of speech.

♦ I am still not sure whether I should quite believe Osip Mandelstam, who considered that the writer was 'a parrot in the deepest sense of the word'. 'A parrot does not belong to any time,' says Mandelstam, 'it does not distinguish day from night. If it bores its owner, the latter will cover it up with a black cloth, and that becomes a surrogate of night for literature.'

Dubravka Ugresic on former Yugoslavia 1993

PATRIOTISM NOW
Felipe Fernández-Armesto

Patriotism is a virtue. It is altruistic: it puts community – the patriot's state or nation – above self. It is progressive, because citizens who want to make their country the best strive to make it better.

And yet, if you are patriotic, I think you shouldn't be. I don't mean that patriotism is a bad thing but that it is surprising in the materialist, atomised, mutable world we inhabit. Globalisation and Europeanisation submerge patriotism, migrations wash over it, devolution re-channels it. Chauvinism and xenophobia embarrass its true adherents and give it a bad name. It seems incredible that patriotism can survive national self-reinvention. Cool Britannia is something you can only be lukewarm about.

Yet patriotism is still around. Focus groups tell the Prime Minister so. Politicians appeal to it, especially when they want to justify wars. Historical parallels show how robust it can be when all around it changes. Robespierre's France, Lenin's Russia, Mao's China all discarded traditional identities with amazing speed and zeal; but patriotism survived – even in ideological environments where it was formally proscribed in favour of internationalism. So what keeps it going in times that ought to quench it? Can it last much longer?

One theory is that patriotism is conditional – a deal you make with the state. States can kid people into patriotism, like any other shuckster, or they can buy it from their citizens at the price of political rights and social welfare. But historically patriotism doesn't seem to be proportionate to the beneficence of the state.

More convincing is the view that patriotism is cultural allegiance, which can survive factual undermining because it's based on myth. But what about when the culture changes, too? In Britain, the stiff upper lip has gone wobbly. Emotional self-indulgence has replaced British reserve. The food has gone foreign. Fair play and the cult of the underdog seem as old-fashioned as warm beer and bowler hats. The class system has yielded to the celeb system. The workshop of the world has been sold off. The Corinthian spirit has vanished from Westminster and Wembley. A lot of green and pleasant land has been drearily redeveloped. The Britain my father wrote about – struggling to understand it, as a foreign visitor, in the 1940s – is barely recognisable today. We have liberal, human, universal values – but you can't erect patriotism, which is an exclusive sentiment, on the basis of universal values. So what's left to be patriotic about?

The problem is particularly acute because we're facing the prospect of war, which will galvanise some people's patriotism and dissolve that of others. It could be patriotic to oppose the war, on the grounds that it would be incompatible with British people's traditionally self-ascribed virtues of fairness, patience and decency. The government, on the other hand, will represent support for 'our boys' as a patriotic obligation. The war lobby's cry sounds uncomfortably like 'My country right or wrong.' But if you pick and choose the values and traditions to which you attach, and adhere to them in defiance of your country, can you call that patriotism?

Meanwhile, devolution, Europeanisation and immigration mean we're living in a country of multiplying loyalties. If historical precedent is anything to go by, Islam and other recently arrived cultural traditions will develop in distinctively British ways and become as British as the House of Windsor. But that's a long-term prospect. What happens in the meantime? Some people might like an environment of perpetual re-negotiation of their allegiances in perpetual transition: it may enhance their sense of freedom. They may want to fight to defend it. This sort of sentiment could, perhaps, replace patriotism. But it can hardly be patriotism. The British lion can't become a chameleon. On the contrary, re-negotiation could adulterate loyalties or create new, conflicting ones, as communities of different ethnic origins define themselves in relation to each other.

This is suggested not only by the fissures that divide some ethnic groups, but also by psychological studies of the way patriotism happens. As we grow up, we don't reject stereotypes of 'alterity' which we acquire in childhood: we multiply them. We classify someone as stereotypically British, say, or 'foreign', and simultaneously as stereotypically working-class, or female, or Muslim, or 'public school', or whatever. Stereotypes function by giving us supposed predictors of the way the people we meet will behave.

So we're psychologically programmed to form allegiances directed against the different. This is why so much residual patriotism gets polluted by nationalism and xenophobia. Is it just an ugly mask, behind which all the real features of patriotism have rotted away? I sometimes think this when I contemplate British people – in the government and on the streets – who seem willing to abandon or abolish their own traditions and historic peculiarities of culture, yet are anxious to impose loyalty-tests on immigrants. I feel it even more intensely when I encounter English louts abroad – people who know so little of their own country that they're aware of nothing to be genuinely proud of: hatred of foreigners is their last refuge, the closest they can get to patriotism.

Perhaps true patriotism will survive if we don't think about it too much, for this is a field in which scrutiny leads to scepticism. Perhaps there are abiding values, concealed at present, which may re-emerge, as they did in Russia or France or China after the revolutions. Patriotism will change because the meaning of Britishness is changing; in the course of change, it may disappear. It may fragment into regional patriotisms or dissolve amid re-negotiation, or vanish into some broader patriotism in a future superstate. For as long as it lasts, it will surely be abused. I suspect it will go on surprising us by its durability: an attachment that has clung to so little for so long clearly has amazing powers of adhesion.

PHOTOGRAPHY

♦ The vulnerability of photography to censorship may reflect our deeply rooted cultural anxieties about the image.

Amy Adler 1996

♦ Privacy is what you get when you are in a private place. Privacy is what you do not get in a public place. For the photographer, anything seen in 'public' can be recorded, but in 'private' the subject's permission is needed.

♦ Lord Wakeham has wacky proposals to protect privacy, proposals that include defining beaches as 'private places'! This should certainly liven them up when consenting adults with an exhibitionist streak get going.

♦ If you have sex with the curtains open, there is no hope of successfully suing a passing photographer. But if a photographer broke into the house to get the picture, he would be punished for trespassing and we would all cheer.

♦ The real invaders of privacy are big business and government. . . . For every person hounded by a paparazzo, a million are photographed in their cars by police and 10 million are video-taped in banks and public buildings. And none of those recorded want to be recorded, whereas most people pursued by paparazzi do.

♦ A symbiotic relationship has always existed between personalities and their paparazzi.

Philip Jones Griffiths on the UK 1997

♦ Malcolm Browne's snapshot of a Buddhist priest immolating himself in a square in Saigon was considered unfit for America's breakfast tables by the editors of the *New York Times*.

♦ In the Gulf War, the *Observer* in London published a gruesome photograph of an incinerated Iraqi staring sightlessly from his truck.

♦ In World War II, I might have hesitated to publish the images of charred bodies after the German bombing of Coventry out of deference to the relatives. Those pictures were suppressed by the government as damaging to morale and in a national crisis that is an argument that deserves some respect – but no too much.

♦ When an authority moves to suppress it is usually an indication that they have little confidence in their actions – precisely when a more informed debate can avert catastrophe. Governments were too ready to suppress pictures from the trenches in World War I. It was a stupid war, and the sooner that everyone realised it the better it would have been.

♦ Propaganda has to be met by propagation of the truth. Tom Hopkinson, the editor of *Picture Post*, was fired because he wanted to publish photographs during the Korean War that his ownership judged 'anti-Western'.

♦ Today an even bigger problem for photography is the ease of manipulation with the computer.

♦ They all of them, censors and manipulators, testify to the power of the still image.

Harold Evans 1999

POLITICAL CORRECTNESS

♦ PC has been pilloried and argued over for more than a decade now. It is all too easy to see how absurd some of its preoccupations are, though it had a sort of utopianism about it, and a touching, if rather authoritarian belief that behaviour, if properly conditioned, will improve. The problem with the ideal of political correctness is that, like so many censorships, it can turn so easily against what it is meant to protect, encouraging everyone to be on guard against everyone else.

Ursula Owen 1998

♦ The nanny philosophy: the view that people's sensitivities must be protected by censorship or suppression of things that might offend them. Such a notion underlies the speech codes adopted at a significant number of American universities in the last 10 years. The codes typically provide for punishment of any student who directs at another insulting comments about the latter's race, religion, gender, sexual orientation and so forth: hate speech, as the backers of codes call it.

♦ David Lodge summed it up well when he said the phrase political correctness 'encapsulates all the dogmatic, puritanical and narrow-minded arrogance that has made people distrust revolutionary politics from Robespierre onwards'.

Anthony Lewis 1995

PORNOGRAPHY

♦ There is no agreed definition of pornography, although it is usually accepted that pornography intends to arouse the reader or viewer sexually, and the bottom line would be that it consists of 'sexually explicit material'. British censorship laws define 'obscene' materials as those that 'tend to deprave and corrupt', but sometimes juries have declared pornography obscene and sometimes they haven't. There have been numerous attempts to distinguish between 'erotica' (good) and 'pornography' (bad) but, like all definitions of porn, there is an inescapably subjective dimension to this. Pornography is controversial because sex is controversial. For all the apparent openness of contemporary culture, sex has not lost its power to disturb: there are competing definitions of what pornography 'is' because these reflect deep-seated conflicts about the purpose and role of sex in modern society.

Elizabeth Wilson 2000

♦ The R18 category is 'a special and legally restricted classification for videos where the focus is mainly on real sexual activity and the purpose is primarily to induce sexual arousal. Erections may be shown, as may a broader range of mild fetish material, but no threats or humiliation or realistic depictions of pain are permitted. There must be no clear sight of penetration, oral, vaginal or anal, or of masturbation. Ejaculation must not be shown.'

British Board of Film Classification 2000

♦ Porn acts as a safety valve, is useful in sex therapy and is educational. Banning porn is an insult to sex.

Tuppy Owens 2000

♦ The argument that it is commercial pornography that underlies the subordination and abuse of women in society is seriously misleading.

Lynne Segal 2000

♦ Pornography is to art as prudery is to the censors.

♦ Pornographic material has been present in the art and literature of every society in every historical period. What has changed from epoch to epoch – or even from one decade to another – is the ability of such material to flourish publicly and to be distributed legally.

♦ As our culture becomes more diverse, we can expect more calls for censorship rather than fewer.

♦ Pornographic art is perceived as dangerous to political movements because, like the unconscious, it is not programmable. It is dangerous play whose outcome never can be predicted. Since dream is the speech of the unconscious, the artist who would create works of value must be fluent in speaking the language of dream. The pornographic has a direct connection to the unconscious.

Erica Jong 1995

♦ Although pornography remains a special realm, its demarcations from acceptable artistic expression have been repeatedly questioned, in ways that define some of the issues of the body and knowledge in our time.

Peter Brooks 1999

♦ A system of dominance and submission, pornography has the weight and significance of any other historically real torture or punishment of a group of people because of a condition of birth.

Andrea Dworkin 1997

♦ Sexual objectification is another characteristic of pornography. It refers to the portrayal of human beings – usually women – as depersonalised sexual things such as 'tits, cunts and ass', not as multi-faceted human beings deserving equal rights with men.

Diana E Russell

POVERTY

♦ 'Everyone has the right to a standard of living adequate for the health and well-being of himself and of his family.'

Universal Declaration of Human Rights Article 25

♦ In 90s America, to be poor is not so much a socio-economic status as it is a serious character flaw.

Mumia Abu-Jamal 1997

♦ Poverty itself is a violation of numerous basic human rights.

Mary Robinson 1998

♦ Globalisation is creating a new geography of poverty. The world's most fundamental abuse of human rights is perpetrated not so much by despotic states, even though they do play a part, as by the world's trading and financial and trading institutions.

Neil Middleton 1998

♦ Today the net worth of the world's 358 richest people is equal to the combined income of the poorest 45% of the world's population – 2.3 billion people.

James Gustave Speth 1996

PRISON

♦ Wei Jingsheng, after over 14 years in prison in China, recently wrote in the *New York Times*: 'There is a tendency on the part of China to view the detention and release of dissidents as a hostage transaction, in which freedom for the prisoner is just a bargaining chip in an economic poker game.'

Joanne Leedom-Ackerman, Sara Whyatt and Mandy Garner 1994

♦ We estimate that about 2,000 writers were imprisoned; that's a conservative figure. Around 1,500 died. Hundreds vanished. Nobody knows what became of them, or where they are buried. All documentation about them was falsified. Their manuscripts are the most important evidence we have.

Vitaly Shentalinsky on the USSR 1991

♦ I write these papers, and then I hide them. They let you write, but every so often they search your cell and take away your writings. They look them over, and after some time they return the ones which are considered permissible. You take them back, and suddenly you loathe them. This system is a diabolical device for annihilating your own soul. They want to make you see your thoughts through their eyes and control them yourself.

♦ Against this method, there are two means of defence. We allow our jailers to take away some of our writings – the ones that express our views unequivocally. Then there are other papers which we prefer to hide – the ones we want to keep for ourselves.

George Mangakis on Greece 1972

PRIVACY

♦ Home Office proposals published in 1999 state that permissible interception should include the breadth of new technology, such as mobile phones, faxes and e-mail. Communication service providers will be compelled to create systems capable of interference (and reasonably assist the authorities when intercepting), all of which will make them less private and secure. In addition, the law will expand to include both public and private networks (such as hotels and workplaces).

♦ Back in 1765, Mr Entick's eloquent lawyer pleaded: 'If they [the search warrants] have been granted by the minister, then it is high time to put an end to them; for if they are held to be legal, the liberty of the country is at an end. Ransacking a man's secret drawers and boxes to come at evidence against him is like racking a body to come at his secret thoughts.' And he won.

Lisa Forrell on the UK 2002

♦ It is likely that within a generation, the DNA of most of the UK population will have been achieved in a national database. In terms of privacy, the Edinburgh policy is momentous. The collection and storage of DNA must surely rank as one of the most intimate invasions of the person, and yet a recent opinion poll suggests that nearly three-quarters of the local population would be willing to give up their DNA in the 'pursuit of a crime'.

♦ Governments and private sector organisations have moved in recent years to incorporate surveillance into almost every aspect of our finances, communication and lifestyle.

♦ Privacy is the right from which all other rights derive.

♦ Details of economically active adults in the developed world are located in around 400 major databases – enough processed data to compile a formidable reference book for each person.

♦ UK InfoDisc has produced a CD-ROM which merges the electoral roll with the telephone book and geodemographic data. So now the most basic and innocent information about you can reveal all manner of additional facts. Your telephone number leads instantly to your address. Your name leads automatically to your occupation and age. It goes without saying that the finance and credit industry, private investigators, newspapers, marketing companies and police all make extensive use of the product.

♦ Much of this technology is used to track the activities of dissidents, human rights activists, journalists, student leaders, minorities, trade union leaders and political opponents.

♦ Hidden cameras – once frowned on – are now being installed unhindered in cinemas, police helmets, pubs, red-light districts, changing rooms and housing estates.

♦ It will be the growth of surveillance in the workplace that will most directly affect people.

♦ Workers in most countries have almost no right to privacy.

♦ Mobile phones are being turned into geographical tracking devices.

♦ However, the most dangerous enemy of privacy is not an interior minister or marketing supremo; it is the well-meaning individual who argues: 'I have nothing to hide, so I have nothing to fear.'

♦ Privacy is the natural partner of freedom of expression. They are equal and compatible rights.

♦ It will become apparent in the coming years that these two rights will form the great pillars of any free society. A genuine and unstinting regard for privacy is the only means to ensure that future generations are protected from the threat of a hostile government, the encroachment of a greedy private sector, or, ironically, the well-intended but thoughtless zeal of fellow citizens.

Simon Davies 2000 and 2001

♦ The surveillance trade is almost indistinguishable from the arms trade. More than 70% of companies manufacturing and exporting surveillance technology also export arms, chemical weapons or military hardware. Surveillance is a crucial element for the maintenance of any non-democratic infrastructure, and an important activity in the pursuit of intelligence and political control.

Privacy International Report 1995

'You have zero privacy – get over it!'

Scott McNealy, CEO Sun Microsystems, quoted by Simon Davies 2000

PROPAGANDA

♦ The fall of the Berlin Wall was also the fall of the last bastion of communist propaganda.

Santiago Kovadloff 1999

♦ Censorship and propaganda are notoriously unreliable tools, prone to spotlight what they seek to conceal, subverting their own objectives with unintended irony.

Mark Thompson 1999

♦ The increasingly key role of the public relations industry in skewing news coverage is singled out.

♦ Chomsky and Herman advance a propaganda model in which there are five major filters through which news must pass 'leaving only the cleansed residue fit to print'. The filters are the size, concentrated ownership, owner wealth and profit orientation of the dominant mass-media firms; advertising as the primary income source of the mass media; media reliance on official sources; 'flak' as a means of disciplining the media; and 'anticommunism' as a national religion and control mechanism.

♦ As Chomsky puts it: 'It's not a matter of how you read . . . People have to understand that there's a major effort being made to manipulate them. That doesn't mean the facts aren't there.'

David Miller 'The media: a user's manual' 1994

♦ With the help of false analogies and mythological generalisations, political propaganda quickly arrives at the rationale of racism, always in defence of the most noble causes, of course.

♦ Propaganda is a virus that makes the one who spreads it sick too.

George Conrad 2000

♦ In 1971, media propaganda succeeded in turning the overwhelming majority of West Pakistan's citizens against the Bengalis: they approved the military government's action in the Eastern province and lost it to Mujib and the Awami League.

A special correspondent 1995

♦ The media sin of omission deminishes our world. The media today is like the frog in the well looking up to see a tiny circle of sky above him, and he thinks that's all there is. We know what we see. In the US, we've had a 50% cut in foreign news – the canvas of coverage is shrinking even as globalisation makes world news vital. Deep in our well, we sing 'we are the world' and believe it.

♦ Pictures can lie – and liars use pictures. Images have become their own imageology. We need to hold the visual media to the same standards of accuracy and credibility as the print media.

Danny Schechter 1999

♦ The prosecutor claims this novel is a piece of propaganda. I take this as an insult to my novel and authorship. I do not write propaganda for anyone and am nobody's instrument. My duty as a writer is to create a kind of literature beyond propaganda and at the service of everyone. I am a writer wed to a literary tradition who, despite everything, has not turned literature into a simple instrument of propaganda.

♦ The duty of good literature is to help man to continue to live and to retain hope, despite injustice and brute force, by reminding him of his humanity. It is not to serve as a weapon in political conflict. The purpose of literary work is always to recall and remind people of fundamental concerns, not to help them forget.

Mehmed Uzun 2001

Q

QUEER

QUEER

♦ The torture and beating of Wyoming college student Matthew Shepard, tied to a fence and left to die, was not a random slaying, but a crime of hate. Shepard was marked for death because he was gay.

♦ Does anyone doubt that the hateful rhetoric of politicians and preachers, no doubt intended 'merely' to stoke a political and fundraising base, ends, too often, in blood?

♦ Even if successful (and no such laws have ever sustained a court challenge) a tighter hate speech regimen would catch the little fish while the big ones swam through the net.

♦ Any political or religious leader who spoke of blacks or Jews in the way that Senators Helms and Lott do about gays would quickly be marginalised.

♦ Until we find a way to impose a similar cost on the most dangerous hate speech of the late 1990s, it will remain unsafe to be gay.

Gara La Marche 1999

♦ In the index to John Boswell's ground-breaking book on homosexuality in the Middle Ages, the entry for 'Translation' says 'see Mistranslation' – or what Boswell, in the text, calls 'the deliberate falsification of historical records'.

Alberto Manguel 1996

♦ The last thing the Jews needed was also to be accused of perversion. To be Jewish was bad enough; to be Jewish and gay, My God! If you suggested that, you'd be something of a masochist.

Lionel Blue 1995

♦ In most of my reading, they were invisible. Mr Pickwick, who saw everyone, never saw them; Monsieur Bovary, who met everyone, never met them; Anna Karenina, who thought she knew everything about her ungracious lover, never noticed them among his acquaintances; they

were absent in Captain Nemo's intimate submarine and on Professor Challenger's expedition to the Lost World. They were never small children like Masie Farange, or adolescents like Holden Caulfield. They never fought in wars like Malraux's heroes or scoured the seas like Captain Ahab. They never became their own nightmares, like Gregor Samsa, or their own happiness, like Beckett's Winnie. Their days were never chronicled, let alone with the minuteness of Leopold Bloom's or Mrs Dalloway's. They lived anonymously and died in unmarked graves. They were those through whose denial our society defined its sexual tenements. They stood behind the door that held this warning: 'Beyond you shall not go.'

♦ This is where the censor's eye is useful. In an effort to condemn, the censor needs to define, however fallaciously, its victim. 'Gay' therefore is everything that in any way presents homosexuality in a favourable light, whether in the telling of a supposedly heterosexual author, or in that of a supposedly homosexual one, who might be considered exemplary simply by writing well. Sometimes it is the recipient who defines – in the censor's eye – the forbidden subject, as when books destined for a gay bookstore are stopped at customs because of their destination. The censor's eye is extraordinarily eclectic.

♦ Since societies define themselves as much by what they include as by what they leave out, acts of censorship belong to the same history as their subjects; they don't supplant them. Gay history extends along a road largely lit by the bonfires of the censors.

♦ Invisibility doesn't mean inexistence.

Alberto Manguel 1995

♦ Gay is a heterosexual concept . . . I'm about as comfortable with the word 'gay' as I am with kiddy porn. I'd prefer to be called a comic. Not a gay comic. Not a queer comic. Not even a gay, queer comic, or a fierce comic, or an alternative comic. It's just the mainstream trying to pigeonhole me, trying to say, OK, he's gay, so it's OK to laugh at his stuff about gays.

Scott Capurro 2000

R

RACE

RAPE

READING

RELIGION

RACE

♦ Race has been a perennial source of discord in science for the past half century, despite the widespread western belief that it has been conclusively discredited as a theme of scientific knowledge.

Marek Kohn 1999

♦ We think of the Ku Klux Klan as selecting isolated black sharecroppers as victims, when, historically, they took aim at blacks who had done too well in business.

Darryl Pinckney 1996

♦ Brazil has the largest black population in the world after Nigeria, yet only 5% of Brazilians (in a recent poll of racial origins) identified themselves as black.

Daniela Cestarollo 1999

♦ Around 60% of young blacks, with no criminal records, have suffered some kind of police brutality . . . Every four hours, a young black is killed in São Paulo.

Primo Preto, Brazilian rap group *Racionas MC's* 1999

♦ Policemen consider blacks as prime suspects in any crime.

Francisco Oliveira on Brazil 1999

♦ From what age do we develop this neanderthal dislike, irritation and hostility towards people of a different tribe or faith, or origin? From childhood? From birth? Or perhaps that is not it, and what I really want to know is how it comes to be there in a person at all.

Anatolii Pristavkin 2000

♦ Anti-racism – the generous inclusion of others into 'we-feeling' and 'we-consciousness' – only becomes the majority sentiment temporarily.

♦ All collective consciousness (religious, national, class, etc) discriminates; discrimination is the fundamental gesture which seeks validation, or an excuse, say, in skin colour, or in a common characteristic of a group.

♦ There are fluid overlaps between patriotism, nationalism, chauvinism, ethnicism, anti-Semitism and racism.

♦ The identity of the enemy is not the determining factor, the essence is hatred of the other, the fellow man.

♦ For the racist, the extinction of the hated group is synonymous with salvation.

George Conrad on Hungary 2000

♦ The challenge today is not to embrace 'difference' as a political goal but to transcend the whole language of race and to put the case for equality.

Kenan Malik 1997

♦ We have put it into law and taken it as wish and necessity that all people are possessed with equal rights. Even Gypsies. In the first class the catechist taught us religion in the following way: 'Love thy neighbour as thyself. Repeat it.' We responded in unison. He levelled a finger at someone and asked, 'Even the Gypsy?' It was a trick question, but the pupil didn't get it. 'No, not the Gypsy,' he answered from out of his clean conscience.

Ludvík Vakulík on the Czech Republic 1998

♦ I think it would be interesting to reprint all the articles in the British press about Romani migration, substituting the word 'Gypsy' with 'Jew', just to see how it looks.

♦ Denigration of the Romani people has been wall-to-wall in the British media. I think *The Times* was alone in printing Gypsy with a capital 'G'; this might seem like a pedantic point were not the slight so deliberate.

♦ Racists have never been able to decide whether to attack immigrants for taking jobs or for living on benefits, and the government seems to have much the same problem.

Jeremy Hardy 1998

♦ In some European stadiums, the spectators screech like chimpanzees at the sight of a black player. Racial integration inside the stadium remains essentially symbolic: athletic stardom is not equivalent to fully human status, let alone equal social status, in the eyes of many Europeans.

John Hoberman 2000

♦ If you're looking for a scapegoat in the US, from Willie Horton to Lani Guinier to Dr Joycelyn Elders, a black person is most convenient. In the face of the persistence and pervasiveness of racism in US society, it is no wonder that many African-Americans find curbs on racist speech an appealing weapon. But it is a boomerang, not a sword.

Gara La Marche 1995

♦ Serious discussion of race has virtually disappeared from British public discourse, surfacing only in spectacular instances where race forces itself on to the media agenda.

Nicola Lacey 1997

RAPE

♦ Rape as a form of violation against women has increasingly entered public awareness. Rape was long seen in popular perception as an individual aberration by men with uncontrollable sexual needs. Its roots in the cultural devaluation of women tended to be ignored or denied. Institutionalised gang-rape is, in fact, culturally sanctioned in parts of Papua New Guinea as a form of control over women. But its appearance as a weapon of war used to humiliate the enemy in a wide variety of contexts is only now being recognised.

Naila Kabeer 1995

♦ Rape does not respect the body of someone else. All types of racism and exclusion are, in the end, ways of denying the body of another. One could reinterpret the entire history of ethics in the light of the rights of the body and the relationship of our body to the rest of the world.

Umberto Eco 1994

♦ If a woman is raped but has no evidence to prove it, the very fact that she had admitted to the sexual act may lead to her own prosecution for adultery or fornication – *zina*.

♦ The zina ordinance was one of a hotch-potch of laws instituted by its then ruler, General Zia ul-Haq, in his attempts to 'islamise' Pakistan in the 1980s. It covers all extra-marital sexual relations, including rape and abduction for the sake of sexual assault. Crimes under zina, as well as rape, are subject to the law's most severe penalities – death by stoning or, in the case of an unmarried person, 100 lashes in public.

♦ Rape in Pakistan is traditionally seen as degrading to the woman and the police treat victims with a mixture of contempt and disbelief.

Valerie Ceccherini 1999

♦ 'Two men from our neighbourhood grabbed me, took me off, beat me and raped me, one after the other. While they were raping and beating me, they took photos. Before letting me go, they told me that if I ever spoke of what had happened, they would kill me, kidnap my daughters and send the photos to the press. My sister-in-law told me not to say anything to my husband: no Pakistani man can accept the idea that this could happen to his wife and she was afraid he would accuse me of having consented to all this and leave me.'

'Some time later, the men who raped me demanded money from me and threatened to show my husband the photos if I didn't give them something. In the end, my husband found out everything and drove me from the house with the children. I went to stay with my father and we filed a charge of rape against the men. It took eight months before the police even registered the charge. When we went to the police station, the police there were abusive to my father and myself. They were so arrogant. One of them said to me: 'You certainly enjoyed yourself with one of them then!' They treated me like a loose woman. They laughed in my father's face and we had to pay 10,000 rupees just to get the charge registered. When the rapists arrived, they treated them quite differently, offering them a seat and something to drink. They arrested one of the men, but he was released with a caution. His accomplices, people of means and influence, were never arrested. While they were at the police station, the rapists confessed, but only verbally; afterwards they bribed the police officers to suppress the confession. And the photos are in the hands of the police: I'm terrified that for another bribe they'd get rid of them as well – the only evidence there is of the crime. A few days ago, a car hit me and I was injured. The drivers said that if I didn't withdraw my charge, the next time would be fatal. The case is still dragging on.'

Pakistani woman rape survivor 1999

READING

♦ The story of my reading, in a succession of book-lined rooms in so many different countries, is also the story of the censorship of my reading.

♦ Over the shoulder of every reader is a censor, praising this, concealing that, distorting something else. At times, the reader submits to this authoritarian judgement; at others, the reader becomes a kabbalist, secretly looking for that which the censor has hidden. Sometimes the censor is grossly obvious, marking off the limits with laws and signs of 'No Trespassing'.

Alberto Manguel 1995

♦ Oesterheld's comic strips were never banned in Argentina; the military didn't find it necessary to ban a book officially to prevent its being read. Reading – that quiet, seemingly private pleasure – became in itself a political act.

Alberto Manguel and Craig Stephenson 1996

RELIGION

♦ 'Everyone has the right to freedom of thought, conscience and religion; this right includes freedom to change his religion or belief, and freedom, either alone or in community with others and in public or in private, to manifest his religion or belief in teaching, practice, worship and observance.'

UN Declaration of Human Rights Article 18

♦ Though the religious parties make a great song and dance, they have no intention whatsoever of allowing people to think or make up their own minds.

Valerie Ceccherini on Pakistan 1999

♦ Millenarianism ought to be respectable: plenty of decent religions with clever, gentle believers started as 'end-is-nigh' cults, including Mormonism, Adventism and good old Christianity. When I got to know some Mormon historians who were attending a conference of their kind at my college in Oxford, I was surprised to find that such admirably rational people were prepared to profess what seemed to me the obvious nonsense of Mormonism: the angelic revelation to Joseph Smith, the lost tablets of gold, Christ's sojourn in America, the self-consciousness of 'latter-day saints'.

♦ In the recent history of Latin America, odious Protestant groups on the extreme right have been willing to collaborate in the destruction of cultures and the exaltation of dictators in their anxiety to prepare the Third World for the Second Coming.

Felipe Fernández-Armesto 2001

♦ Liberation Theology is a theory that articulates the liberating practice of the church, expressed in a preferential option for the poor, both in the fight against poverty and in favour of their freedom.

Leonardo Boff on Brazil 1999

♦ There are religions of love and religions of hate, it is not likely that either will disappear from the face of the earth and from people's hearts, they just remake themselves, find new targets, update their vocabularies and tool kits.

George Conrad 2000

♦ Communities separated into 'them' and 'us', religion became the marker of identity, borders were suddenly drawn across villages and communities.

Urvashi Butalia on India 1997

♦ There seems to be no possibility of compromise between the two standpoints, the liberal and the authoritarian, whether Christian, Muslim or Jewish, and there is no way in which the two contrasting sets of beliefs can somehow be welded together and combined. Perhaps there will always be persons, and even whole populations, who ignore any clear formulation of the two sets of opposing beliefs and who do not recognise, or do not acknowledge, the impossibility of combining them. They have a way of life which requires that they do not raise questions about the compatibility of the beliefs about free expression which allegedly guide their actions. In fact they do not attach much importance to beliefs as such, and therefore they do not trouble themselves with any reflective evaluation of them.

♦ There are several reasons to believe that clashes between these bitterly opposed moral standpoints will become even more frequent in the coming decades than they have been in the past. The recent elections in Algeria, with Muslim fundamentalists at the top of the poll, point one probable way to the future. Within Algeria the French-educated and deeply secular middle class will be asked to share their political and legal institutions with devout Muslim believers who wish to detach Algeria from the traditions of the French Revolution and of its liberal and free-thinking aftermath. As loyalty to the revolutionary ideals of socialism has declined, religious enthusiasm will tend to take its place. It seems altogether contrary to what is known about human nature, as it has been revealed in history, to expect that, suddenly, populations, when released from Marxist dogmatism and political enthusiasm, will turn to a disillusioned scepticism or to liberal principles. The great inequalities of opportunity within ordinary capitalism, and the ugly effects of the scramble for wealth which it engenders, are still hateful to the unsuccessful crowds in the streets.

♦ As socialism associated itself with nationalist feeling, so also religious enthusiasm associates itself with the repudiation of foreign influences and of cosmopolitan customs. A whole new morality is institutionalised and imposed by an authoritarian government: new sexual conventions, new family structures, new forms of censorship, new undemocratic procedures in government. A fundamentalist revolution involves as great a transformation of the social order as the Communist revolutions which preceded it.

♦ The hostility between free-thinking liberals and religious fundamentalists has a metaphysical basis and is likely to be more long-lasting. The split may even represent an opposition within human nature which is permanent and which cannot be expected to disappear.

Stuart Hampshire 1992

♦ Nehru saw that religion had the potential to divide rather than unite people and this was anathema to him.

Sidharth Bhatia on India 2002

♦ We've got to a point where some clerics think they have a right to say whatever they like about religion. It's not clear who has given them this right.

♦ In a religious community, any kind of reform must begin with religious reform.

♦ Freedom must go hand in hand with being better informed and understanding more and better.

♦ The language of rights must replace the language of duties.

Abdol Karim Soroush on Iran 2002

♦ The Christian Right is a movement of resentment, which makes it available to extremist manipulation.

♦ It is said that in the last days of the earth the pages of every copy of the Quran will go blank. No doubt the Bible will go on talking. A country deserves the extremists it gets.

Darryl Pinckney on the US 1996

♦ Rather like the Soviet Communist Party, the Orthodox Church is a nation-wide club offering a badge, community, social security and support. Religious loyalties, like tribal ones, offer welcome distinctions in times when familiar cultural and geopolitical outlines shift or fade.

♦ Meanwhile a flood of foreign missionaries, 30,000 strong, is swamping the new 'dark continent' with Bibles, junk publicity . . . and promises of study trips to the West.

Irena Maryniak on Russia 1996 and 1999

♦ There is little ground for believing the secular right will prevent the unholy alliance between nationalism and religious fundamentalism.

Baruch Kimmerling on Israel 1996

♦ The illiberal fundamentalist, like the convinced communist before him, can be in one of two situations: either he lives in a society, roughly to be called totalitarian, in which fundamental moral questions are settled by authority or by force and are beyond dispute; or he lives in a society within which a formidable number of its citizens will not agree that fundamental moral questions are beyond dispute. Then the fundamentalist must either resort to force, on the assumption that he is powerful enough to suppress all free expression; or he must enter into public arguments, so far accepting the canons of argument which govern adversary procedures. He is led into a public display of rationality by the existence of fellow citizens who reject the route to moral certainty through a supernatural and superior authority. He must either live alone with his fellow believers and not venture out into the world beyond the Pale, or play a part in the institutions which are established for adversary argument – such institutions as the law courts, the press, parliaments, assemblies, councils and party meetings. This is the point at which mutual awareness, with the new means of communication, becomes relevant. It is becoming always more difficult to segregate the believers in a faith from full knowledge of, and normal dealings with, the rest of humanity.

Stuart Hampshire 1992

S

SAMIZDAT   **SEX**

SCIENCE   **SILENCING**

SECRECY   **SLAVERY**

SAMIZDAT

♦ The last few years have seen the appearance among the intelligentsia and our young people of certain ideologically corrupting documents in the form of political, economic and philosophical essays, literary works, open letters to government, Party, the judiciary or prosecutor, and memoirs written by those claiming to be 'victims of the personality cult'. Those who write and distribute these texts call them 'literature outside censorship' or *samizdat* [self-publishing].

♦ In most cases, this samizdat is a typed or hand-written manuscript, passed from hand to hand and reproduced on photocopiers and duplicating machines. The distribution of these works attracts shady types and speculators who make a profit by selling them and holding on to the proceeds.

♦ The information contained in their samizdat is largely used by capitalist intelligence organisations and foreign anti-Soviet groups in their campaigns against the USSR.

♦ Imperialist reactionaries consider samizdat one of the ways in which they can weaken socialist society within our country and give the authors and distributors of these politically damaging documents all possible support.

Yuri Andropov 1995

♦ The original imaginary film, *We Live not Feeling the Land Beneath our Feet,* was followed by *Free Speech II, From Samizdat to Glasnost.* It portrayed an author who, the moment he had finished writing an article, a book, a poem not entirely loyal to the authorities, meticulously took one carbon copy from the typewriter, wrapped it in polythene and buried it in the snow. Other copies were given to friends to hide. Finally, one was circulated from person to person and, from that moment, the work began a life of its own. It might cross the state frontier of the USSR – with or without its author's knowledge – and return as a published book. We needed no reminder of the likely fate of its author should that happen.

Larisa Bogoraz 2002

♦ Samizdat may be said to constitute a peculiar species of publishing since about 1966. At first, many *belles lettres* appeared by way of samizdat. Later this channel was used for disseminating materials of a political nature. The authors are frequently, but not exclusively, dissidents or persons speaking on behalf of national and religious minorities or other groups. A common motive of those who engage in samizdat is to evade the limits imposed by governmental censorship.

Dietrich A Loeber 1973

♦ In 1972, the year *Index* first appeared, Alexander Ginzburg succeeded in compiling a transcript of the trial of Andrei Siniavskii that he circulated in samizdat – typing out copies with ever fainter carbon paper and circulating them among friends.

♦ A chain process was launched which led to the *Chronicle of Current Events,* a samizdat journal that baldly recorded instances of the Soviet authorities violating their own laws in dealing with their own citizens.

♦ Another product of the chain process was *Index on Censorship* itself.

Geoffrey Hosking 2002

SCIENCE

♦ In truth, although science should not be an ideology, it has often clashed with ideologies; and it still does, in ways both obvious and subtle. In Stalin's Russia, Mendel's genetics seemed to clash with Marxist ideology. Mendelian genetics says that all creatures, including humans, inherit much of their basic character, while Marx was perceived to argue that all creatures, including humans, can be changed at will by manipulating their environment. Great Russian geneticists were suppressed, charlatans flourished. Nikolai Ivanovitch Vavilov made immense contributions to plant breeding and, for his pains, ended his days in a Siberian labour camp.

♦ Most sinister, are the many barriers that inhibit and distort the flow of notions from the scientist to people at large. All policy-makers, and all citizens in a democracy worthy of the name, need to know what is going on; and, for all kinds of reasons, we don't.

Colin Tudge 1999

♦ The public fears that biogenetics will produce Frankenstein products – apples that will devour Devon. But the deeper threat of biogenetic engineering is this massive expansion of censorship required for the new industry to succeed. Monsanto is the perfect McLuhan company. Its true product is information. That the information is imprinted inside a seed or bacterium's DNA, as opposed to newsprint or web page, is not significant.

♦ In much of the world this valuable tool, censorship, remains a government monopoly.

♦ What we see in Monsanto's controlling exposure of information about their products is the new trend toward privatisation of censorship.

Gregory Palast 1999

SECRECY

♦ Access to the Lubianka is strictly controlled . . . At the Lubianka they have a military sort of mentality. The files are marked 'strictly confidential' and sometimes they'll say: 'There's nothing secret here, but by law we don't have the right to show it to you. When the Supreme Soviet repeals the law you're most welcome to look.' And the Supreme Soviet is dragging its feet. Why? Pressure from the Party. The KGB still has more respect for the views of the Party than for the Congress of People's Deputies. Old laws paralyse us. It's the same with economics, ideology, culture . . .

Vitaly Shentalinsky on the USSR 1991

♦ The secrecy surrounding the [early days of the] Soviet space programme extended even to those favoured foreigners allowed to participate.

Vera Rich 1999

♦ The Scott Report is the most important constitutional document to appear in Britain this century. It exposes the lack of openness in government; the contempt of ministers for their constitutional responsibility to inform Parliament and the public of their actions and be held accountable for them; the plethora of so-called 'gagging' devices preventing access to government documents and the total lack of accountability within the Civil Service. Scott is categorical: it was not 'national security' or the 'public interest' that caused government to engage in its tissue of deception and evasion: it was fear of 'public opinion' likely to condemn the cynical arming of a murderous dictator whose British weaponry had already murdered his own people and, only months later, would be turned on British troops in the Gulf War.

Judith Vidal-Hall 1996

♦ Of course, our government has many, many secrets which our enemies always seem to know about in advance but our people are not told of until years later, if at all.

Gore Vidal on the US 2002

♦ The reasons the Israeli authorities kept my brother's kidnapping and trial a total secret are the same as those that keep their nuclear weapons production taboo.

Meir Vanunu 1991

♦ It remains an unhappy fact of British life that all journalistic enterprises continually come up against the barriers of secrecy erected by the powerful in their attempts to prevent the public being told.

Michael Grade 1994

SEX

♦ The inclusion, for its own sake, of erotic material in a free-to-air television service is a step change in the use of sex on British television and begins to erode the other difference . . . between what is available on open access channels and that which is available through pay services. The Commission also considers that their inclusion in a mainstream television service runs the risk of encouraging both the amount of such material and the erosion of standards generally.

Bulletin of the Broadcasting Standards Commission 1999

♦ Large numbers of books continue to be banned in China. These include titles such as *Ancient Crime: Report on the Sale of Women,* published in 1989 and banned as 'pornographic'; *Collection on Chinese Women,* ordered to be destroyed in 1990 for 'problems in thinking and content', *Memorandum on Marriage and Sex in Contemporary China,* banned in 1990 because one of the essays in the book was said to advocate 'attitudes to sexual liberation and freedom'.

Urvashi Butalia 1996

♦ Sex education publications have suffered at the hands of censors, but it has been a murky picture and I would suggest there have been elements of self-censorship on the part of health educators.

Lynne Walsh on the UK 1996

♦ Sex grabs the attention, and TV schedulers are aware of this. It is the apparently increasing reliance on sex in their programming which has consistently attracted the attentions of the television regulators over the past year – with censure on occasion leading to self-censorship.

♦ The BSC's annual *Monitoring Report* showed that, when asked whether violence, bad language or sex on television caused them most concern, 58% cited violence, 24% bad language and 12% sex. Asked if the amount of sex on television was too much/about right/too little, 38% said 'too much'. This compared with 32% the previous year, but to 41% in 1991, 1992 and 1996 – hardly a rising tide of concern.

Julian Petley on the UK 2000

SILENCING

♦ There are two sorts of silence. There is the silence when no one utters and there is the silence when no one hears.

♦ Of course it is possible to stop someone speaking. The most efficient way of doing so is to kill them. Or you can frighten someone into 'voluntary' silence; render it physically impossible for someone to speak by, for instance, cutting out their tongue or cauterising their brain; impose such powerful cultural taboos that something quite literally becomes unspeakable – as, for instance, the name of God in Jewish religion.

♦ Much censorship works by preventing the would-be speakers from using any channel of public communication.

♦ There is an alarming tendency in the silenced to develop new and creative channels of communication. Procne had her tongue cut out to prevent her revealing her brother-in-law's incestuous and adulterous rape, so she took to embroidery; Russian dissidents generated *samizdat* texts; prisoners in isolation cells tap on metal pipes.

Sara Maitland 2001

♦ When I found out my husband was HIV positive they told me not to tell anybody, not even my mother. My mother in-law threatened me that if I told my family she would chase me out of their home.

♦ But it was good that I talked, because I think it made me strong. I felt I had got rid of some of my stress. Other people, they keep it in their hearts and don't talk about it, and they get ill from the stress.

Stembiso on Aids in Zimbabwe 2000

♦ There is a deafening silence on the Nazi period; an impenetrable wall, thicker even than in Germany. There can be no contrition because nobody is to blame. Above all, let no one destroy the myth of Austria as victim!

Yossi 2000

♦ One can hear no voices / Yet the silence deafens, the guarded ones have sent the word: / Please guard us from the guardians.

Zoran Filipovic, Bosnian writer and photographer 1995

♦ I am still troubled by a sense of incompleteness. Nothing that can be written or spoken is as ambiguous as silence, and I am troubled by this silence. I return to my work and to my life but at the back of my mind I ask myself whether this silence indicates a contemptuous indifference, a shiftiness, a tiny unease or a bureaucratic prudence. Perhaps it is not the endless silence which follows the last line of a dialogue, but merely a pause, a very long pause. I would still like to return to Prague, and this desire has become an end in itself, independent of any reason for going. Whether I go purely as a tourist for another look at the castle, whether I go to shake the hands of a few people who have fallen from grace and to reaffirm, uselessly, that they have not been entirely forgotten and ignored, or whether I go to have my bourgeois moral scruples corrected by someone in authority, the idea of going back, and the sense of frustration, remain with me. I have had no luck with official channels. Perhaps I'll have more luck with a sideways attempt herewith, therefore, my final application for a visa to visit the Czechoslovak Socialist Republic.

Tom Stoppard 1981

SLAVERY

♦ There are something like 111 million [children like Shiva] in India, roughly 12% of the population – child labourers sold, often by their own families, into a form of slavery that has come to be known as bonded labour.

Urvashi Butalia 1997

♦ The Indian government enacted a law: the Regulation and Abolition of Child Labour Act. How can you regulate something you want to abolish? The moment you speak of regulation of slavery, you're recognising something, giving it legal status.

Vassudha Daghamvar 1997

♦ If you insist on defining slavery as 'the legal ownership of one person by another' then slavery has pretty well disappeared. But the key is not ownership, but control through violence. In the 5,000 years of human civilisation, slavery has been a constant, sometimes a form of ownership, sometimes not. Part of our ignorance rests on this confusion about what slavery is.

♦ There is an irreducible core to slavery: violence. The control of one person by another through violence (or its threat) is the constant attribute of slavery throughout history. Couple that with an economic exploitation in which someone is paid nothing and you have a good working definition of the new slavery that encompasses about 27 million people around the world.

♦ With the large numbers of vulnerable people and the low cost of violence, slaves are inexpensive. In 1850, an average agricultural slave in Alabama sold for US$1,000, around US$40,000 in today's money.

♦ It costs about US$2,000 to enslave a young woman into a brothel in Thailand. Once there she will generate as much as US$75,000 profit each year.

♦ There are around 35,000 enslaved prostitutes in Thailand, generating a yearly profit of US$1.85 billion.

♦ Sex tourists spend an estimated US$26.2 billion a year – 13 times more than Thailand earns from any one of its major industries.

♦ Citizens of 74% of countries with high international debt load are regularly trafficked into slavery (the figure for countries with low international debt load is 29%).

Kevin Bales and Humfrey Hunter 2000

♦ Sometimes you can find three generations on one farm working in bondage. Sometimes they are kept in chains, under the surveillance of armed guards.

Ali Hassan on Pakistan 2000

♦ Systems of slave labour continue to exist in China. As a survivor of the Chinese forced labour camp system – the Laogai – I can testify to the excruciating ways in which I was reduced to an instrument of the state and forced to work under deplorable conditions to line the pockets of those in control.

Harry Wu 2000

♦ If you want to keep your slave docile, you can beat her regularly and savagely, cut her with a knife, drug her, rape her or burn her with cigarettes. On the other hand, if physical violence reduces her value, you can rely on threats to turn her in as an illegal immigrant or a fake refugee, to mutilate or kill her, or to visit some terrible harm on her family.

Alan Hope on East European traffickers in women 2000

♦ If slavery is a state of having others take all-important decisions about your life, owing obligations to others with no hope that you can ever pay them off, working for others without fair recompense and with no end in sight, being in danger of severe punishment if you try to escape and suffering a prohibition against organising with other people with similar problems, then the external debt of poor countries today is a form of slavery.

Bob Sutcliffe 2000

T

TECHNOLOGY
TERRORISM
TOLERANCE
TORTURE
TRANSLATION
TRUTH &
RECONCILIATION

TECHNOLOGY

♦ Technology frequently outpaces the scope of existing moral frameworks intended to restrict and contain it.

British Medical Association 1999

♦ Sometimes it is hard not to sympathise with latter-day Canutes attempting to hold back the waves pouring down from the sky; what has been aptly called 'electronic imperialism' will sweep away much that is good, as well as much that is bad. Yet it will only accelerate changes that were in any case inevitable and, on the credit side, the new media will preserve for future generations the customs, performing arts and ceremonies of our time in a way that was never possible in any earlier age.

Arthur C Clarke 1995

♦ The digital revolution offers a new democracy, dominated neither by the vested interests of political parties nor the mob's baying howl. It can narrow the gap that separates capital from labour; it can deepen the bonds between the people and the planet.

♦ But the truth is that information and communications technology can add nothing to a society that wields low expectations for what humanity can achieve offline.

♦ The internet typifies post-Cold War society. . . which involves masses of people but brings them together as individuals.

♦ Information Communication Technologies (ICTs) are neither the cause nor the solution to today's social problems.

Chris Ellison 1999

♦ Satellite was not like other television. As Murdoch has remarked: 'In the end technology can get past politicians and regulators.'

Christopher Hird 1994

TERRORISM

♦ Any threat or use of violence to terrorise or intimidate civilians for political ends counts as terrorism.

♦ Those who say you cannot stop terror with military force don't know what language terror speaks. It understands and respects only force.

♦ Now, as the new Cold War against terror begins, the same balancing act will be required. We shall have to balance moral conviction with sustained thinking about what policies, what actions, will or will not work.

♦ The fundamental sin of terrorism is not just that it kills and maims innocent human beings: it corrupts faith in the possibility of rational, ie peaceful, political change.

Michael Ignatieff 2002

♦ Voices within the US have accused it of censoring what it labelled 'dangerous' images and leaving its population with only the iconic, and in the end defiant, remains of their two towers imprinted on their consciousness in the interests of maintaining public morale and consumer spending, and preventing a stock-market crash.

♦ Death by terror does not have a face, only a symbol. It's a new version of the body-bag syndrome.

Judith Vidal-Hall on 9/11 2001

♦ The Senate rushed through counter-terrorism legislation that would drastically abridge rights of free speech, association, due process, fair trial and privacy . . . the proposed new anti-terrorist legislation does not make us more safe, only less free.

Nadine Strossen 1995

♦ The UK Prevention of Terrorism Act of 1973 (PTA) was renowned among activists and lawyers as one of the most rights-abusive pieces of legislation on the statute book. The 19 February 2001 Terrorism Act's definition of terrorism, and its extension to acts that take place outside this country, pose serious threats to freedom of expression, freedom of association and the right of asylum.

Claire Fauset 2001

♦ Police State? What's that all about? In April 1996, one year after the Oklahoma city bombing, President Clinton signed into law the Anti-Terrorist and Effective Death Penalty Act, a so-called 'conference bill' in which many grubby hands played a part including the bill's co-sponsor, Senate majority leader Bob Dole.

♦ But faced with opposition to anti-terrorism legislation, Clinton attacked his critics as 'unpatriotic'.

Gore Vidal 2002

♦ In December 2002, the UK Parliament introduced new anti-terrorism laws under which suspects can be detained, indefinitely, without trial. Using its commanding majority, Tony Blair's government has reversed, in six weeks, principles that have underpinned the UK's legal system for four centuries.

♦ It has passed without demur laws that would have delighted Stalin or Beria.

Mark Fisher 2002

♦ The US military and world terrorists seem to be maintaining a symbiotic relationship. It's not surprising that both sides share the same basic narrative explanation for the violence: evil versus good.

Mark Pedelty 2002

♦ If the world is to be spared what future historians may call the 'Century of Terror', we shall have to chart the perilous course between the Scylla of US imperial arrogance and the Charybdis of Islamic religious fanaticism.

Pervez Hoodbhoy 2002

◆ Since 12 September, I've asked people in my office [The Organisation for Security and Cooperation in Europe] not to use the word 'terrorist'. It's a dangerous word: it can stigmatise anyone, whether or not that person has been tied to any criminal act. You can point the finger at an enemy without going into details. Any imprecision encourages people to put everything into the same bag and licenses excess. The media is to some extent responsible for this; they should have described bin Laden as a criminal assassin and not gone hook, line and sinker for this 'terrorism' business.

Freimut Duve 2002

◆ A raft of extreme measures, originally designed to target an emergency situation, is to be reinforced and made permanent despite the ending of that specific emergency. In the 1974 Act terrorism was defined as 'the use of violence for political ends including any use of violence for the purpose of putting the public, or any section of the public in fear'. In 1999's Bill, terrorism had become 'the use of serious violence against persons or property, or the threat to use such violence, to intimidate or coerce a government, the public or any section of the public for political, religious or ideological ends.'

Frank Fisher on the UK 2000

TOLERANCE

◆ The boundaries of the intolerable cross over clearly discernible thresholds. Take, for example, this business of revisionism. I see nothing shocking in a serious and incontrovertible work establishing that the figure for genocide of the Jews by the Nazis was not 6 million but 6.5 or 5.5 million. What is intolerable is when something which might have been a work of research no longer has the same meaning and worth, and becomes a message suggesting that 'if a few less Jews than we thought were killed, there was no crime'.

◆ To be tolerant, one must set the boundaries of the intolerable.

♦ I do not want to use the word 'true'. There are only opinions, some of which are preferable to others. Our life and that of others hangs on this word preferable. One can die for an opinion which is only preferable.

Umberto Eco 1994

♦ In a lecture, Dr Carey, Archbishop of Canterbury, condemns Salman Rushdie's 'outrageous slur' on the Prophet Mohammed in *The Satanic Verses* and says: 'Tolerance is achieved when people hold their religion as so important that to part from it is to die, and at the same time realise that another person's values are just as important and as real.'

Fiction, Fact and the Fatwa: A Chronology of Censorship

♦ Several democracies have adopted laws and 'speech codes' censoring racist or other forms of hate speech that we properly despise: German law, for example, makes it a crime to deny the existence of the Holocaust. These campaigns and laws are particularly attractive in Western democracies because they urge censorship in the interests not of the powerful but of the vulnerable; in the name not of injustice but of equality. They must nevertheless be resisted because if we deny freedom of speech to opinions we hate, we weaken the legitimacy of our entire political system, particularly the legitimacy of the very laws we pass to protect victims of stereotype and prejudice.

Ronald Dworkin 1997

♦ I had always presumed that fear is what breeds violence, but I had known it only in theory, and now I had witnessed that theory incarnated in a real human being. I had been the potential victim of that fear, had seen the violence disappear as the fear itself melted in front of my eyes, had survived because I was able to convince the soldier that I was neither dangerous nor different. My words broke the isolating circle he had drawn around himself. I had used words to contact his humanity and stimulate his empathy, I had used our common vocabulary to place his skin in my skin and his eyes inside my eyes, to feel the world from my perspective. What art, what literature does: children who dance together find it difficult to slaughter one another in the streets.

Ariel Dorfman 1997

TORTURE

♦ As happens in the great Shakespearean tragedies, the most painful scenes are juxtaposed sometimes with scenes of ridiculous farce. A scene of torture is a scene of inhuman tragedy. But the infinite bestiality of the seven orang-utans who tortured me created an absurd dialogue of the deaf.

♦ My torturer said: 'You're right. I am torturing you. But since you are an artist, since you are well-known and appear on television from time to time, I am torturing you, I give you that, but I am torturing you with respect.'

Agusto Boal on Brazil 1999

♦ The torturer is a functionary. The dictator is a functionary. They are armed bureaucrats and they lose their job if they don't do it efficiently. There is no more to it than that. They are not extraordinary monsters. We are not going to give them that distinction.

♦ The first death as a result of torture unleashed – in Brazil in 1964 – a national scandal. The tenth death by torture was barely reported in the press. The fiftieth was accepted as 'normal'. The machine teaches people to accept horror in the same way that one gets used to the cold in winter.

Eduardo Galeano 1978

♦ A CNN poll in 2001 revealed that 45% of Americans would not object to the use of torture if it provided information about terrorism.

Ursula Owen 2002

♦ The purpose of torturing is to get their responses. It's not something we do for fun. We must hurt them so that they respond quickly. Another purpose is to break them and make them lose their will. It's not something that's done out of individual anger, or for self-satisfaction. So we beat them to make them afraid, but absolutely not to kill them . . . Don't be so bloodthirsty that you cause their death quickly. You won't get the needed information.

Khmer Rouge Interrogator's manual 1986

TRANSLATION

♦ Don't fixate on a word, consult and glide on, be mobile and come back to it later. When you feel pain in the words, be grateful for the writer suffered it for you, for us; and know that a love poem is a singular gift to you the translator: to open, admire and give on to the reader.

Richard McKane 2002

♦ In the early Middle Ages, translation (from the past participle of the Latin *trasferre*, 'to transfer') meant conveying the relics of a saint from one place to another. Carrying away something precious and making it one's own by whatever means possible: this definition of translation serves the act of literary translation as well.

♦ Were translation a simple act of pure exchange, it would offer no more possibilities for distortion and censorship than photocopying.

♦ Throughout the nineteenth century, the classic Greek and Roman texts were recommended for the moral education of women only when purified in translation.

♦ It is possible to censor not only a word or a line of text through translation, but also an entire culture.

♦ Translating into the tongue of the conqueror always carries within the act the danger of assimilation or annihilation; translating into the tongue of the conquered, the danger of overpowering or undermining.

♦ In our days, censorship in translation takes place under more subtle guises. In certain countries, authors are still submitted to cleansing purges.

♦ Not all translation, however, is corruption and deceit. Sometimes cultures can be rescued through translation, and translators become justified in their laborious and menial pursuits.

Alberto Manguel 1996

♦ **3 July 1991** In Milan, Ettore Capriolo, 61, Italian translator of *The Satanic Verses*, is beaten and repeatedly stabbed by a man claiming to be Iranian, who demands Salman Rushdie's address. Ettore Capriolo translated the book in 1989 for the Mondadori publishing house and had been given police protection for several months during 1990 after receiving threats from Islamic fundamentalists.

11 July 1991 In Tokyo, Professor Hitoshi Igarashi, Japanese translator of *The Satanic Verses*, is stabbed to death at Tsukuba University. A spokesman for the Pakistan Association in Japan says: 'the murder was completely, 100% connected with the book . . . Today we have been congratulating each other. Everyone was really happy'.

12 July 1991 Salman Rushdie issues a statement: 'I am extremely distressed by the news of the murder of Mr Hitoshi Igarashi, and I offer my condolences and deepest sympathy to his family. Only a few days ago, Mr Ettore Capriolo, the Italian translator of *The Satanic Verses*, narrowly survived a similar, horrifying attack. It is hard to avoid linking the two events.'

12 July 1991 The Swedish PEN Centre, together with the Swedish Writers' and Translators' Association, condemns the assassination of Salman Rushdie's Japanese translator: 'Such abhorrent acts of violence pose a threat against the freedom of expression and against the important role of translators as intermediaries of thoughts and ideas across borders'.

14 July 1991 Laiqat Hussain, President of Bradford's Council of Mosques, says that Ayatollah Khomeini's original *fatwa* applies to anyone involved in publishing *The Satanic Verses* . 'These people who have translated cannot get away with it. That is the position. There will be repercussions. Even if it means death.'

18 July 1991 The Japan PEN Club issues a statement following the murder of Professor Igarashi, translator of *The Satanic Verses*: 'if this atrocity is connected with the translation of this book, it would be a grave threat to the freedom of expression set forth in the Charter of the International PEN and a fearful violation of basic human rights. If this atrocious crime was committed for such a reason, it cannot be tolerated, regardless of any consideration of religious differences, and the Japan PEN Club, as an organisation devoted to promoting mutual understanding among different cultures, expresses its deep sorrow and sincere condolences on the tragic death of Professor Igarashi'.

Fiction, Fact and the Fatwa: A Chronology of Censorship

TRUTH & RECONCILIATION

♦ 'Everyone is entitled to a social and international order in which the rights and freedoms set forth in this declaration can be fully realised.'

Universal Declaration of Human Rights Article 28

♦ 'Without truth, especially where there have been serious human rights atrocities, there cannot be any enduring peace or any reconciliation.'

Richard Goldstone on War Crimes Tribunals 1995

♦ Many documents have been destroyed and it can be very hard to find your way around. If we were to publish everything without analysing it first, the falsification would be permanent. We have to try to glean the truth, and for that you have to work with a certain institution . . .

♦ People are still very ignorant. The Soviet era was deeply traumatic. We were dragged into barbarism, and when we finally emerged we found we had to learn how to live anew. Each and every one of us. To start living afresh you have to remember who you are and that you have a history. Ah yes . . . we had a Tsar once . . . and perhaps not everything he did was entirely wrong . . .

Vitaly Shentalinsky on USSR 1991

♦ Media clichés about reconciliation and humanisation invariably run counter to traditional beliefs that monsters only fake their rehabilitation and will inevitably revert to true character.

♦ Reconciliation is impossible without full knowledge of what you are being reconciled to.

Stanley Cohen 2000

♦ Forgiveness and reconciliation has a price tag attached to it.

♦ If you do not open up and examine that can of worms now, in a controlled environment, that can of worms is going to open some day. And we shall remain in an unstable environment because you will never know when some revelation is going to happen.

♦ There is no distinction between someone who is a victim of human rights violations, perpetrated by, say, the liberation movements, or one who is a victim of violations perpetrated by the apartheid dispensation.

Archbishop Desmond Tutu 1996

♦ Fifty years after the Nuremberg Trials, South Africans stand on the eve of their Truth and Reconciliation Commission. The search for the truth about the past. The demand for the guilty to step forward. To be forgiven? To be punished? A former apartheid minister takes the stand. He peers at the watching Commissioners. 'Comrades,' he says, his moustache twitching. 'I have a clear conscience. I have never used it!'

♦ So how can a Truth Commission find any truth, when we have no-one who admits to the lies? How can we find guilt when all the evidence has been destroyed? Files have been shredded, names have been changed. A past has been forgotten. A nation stares into the future, lobotomised by soccer fever and embracing amnesia like a child a fluffy toy.

♦ But I think there will also be much bitter laughter, as we see those who parade their designer innocence trip over their own nooses of deception.

♦ When we look back to those bad years when the lights of our civilisation seemed to be out forever, one can see how Truth, as we think we know it today, passed through three stages. First it was ridiculed, and as a result the bearers of that truth were imprisoned, banned and killed. Then it was opposed as being the Lie, the subversion of goodness, the Satan! And now it is regarded as self-evident!

♦ A sinister minister of police during the 1980s said it all, as only they could: 'The public is entitled to know what is happening around it. But at the same time, it is equally entitled to the Truth.'

♦ Same old story. Truth is rarely pure and never simple! And 50 years after the Nuremberg Trials, will we see history not just repeating itself, but taking tragedy and turning it into farce?

Pieter-Dirk Uys 1996

♦ The function of truth commissions, like the function of honest historians, is simply to purify the argument, to narrow the range of permissible lies.

♦ What does it mean for a nation to come to terms with its past? Do nations, like individuals, have psyches? Can a nation's past make a people ill as we know repressed memories sometimes make individuals ill? Conversely, can a nation or contending parts of it be reconciled to their past, as individuals can, by replacing myth with fact and lies with truth? Can we speak of nations 'working through' a civil war or an atrocity as we speak of individuals working through a traumatic memory or event?

♦ The War Crimes Tribunal in The Hague is collecting evidence about atrocities in the former Yugoslavia. It is doing so not simply because such crimes against humanity must be punished – otherwise international humanitarian law means nothing – but also because establishing the truth about such crimes through the judicial process is held to be crucial to the eventual reconciliation of the people of the Balkans. In the African city of Arusha, a similar tribunal is collecting evidence about the genocide in Rwanda, believing likewise that truth, justice and reconciliation are indissolubly linked in the rebuilding of shattered societies.

♦ In Tutu's own words, the aim is 'the promotion of national unity and reconciliation . . . the healing of a traumatised, divided, wounded, polarised people'. Laudable aims, but are they coherent?

♦ Such articles of faith inspired the truth commissions in Chile, Argentina, Brazil that sought to find out what had happened to the thousands of innocent people killed or tortured by the military juntas during the 1960s and 1970s. All these commissions believed that if the truth were known, a people made sick by terror and lies would be made well again.

♦ The record of the truth commissions in Latin America has disillusioned many of those who believed that shared truth was a precondition of social reconciliation.

♦ The societies in question used the truth commissions to indulge in the illusion that they had put the past behind them.

♦ The German writer and thinker Theodor Adorno observed this false reconciliation at work in his native Germany after the war: Coming to terms with the past' does not imply a serious working through of the past, the breaking of its spell through an act of clear consciousness. It suggests, rather, wishing to turn the page and, if possible, wiping it from memory. The attitude that it would be proper for everything to be forgiven and forgotten by those who were wronged is expressed by the party that committed the injustice.'

♦ A truth commission cannot overcome a society's divisions. It can only winnow out the solid core of facts upon which society's arguments with itself should be conducted.

♦ The idea that reconciliation depends on shared truth presumes that shared truth about the past is possible. But truth is related to identity. What you believe to be true depends, in some measure, on who you believe yourself to be. And who you believe yourself to be is mostly defined in terms of who you are not.

Michael Ignatieff 1996

♦ If we believe we are fighting for the truth, we are sometimes tempted to kill our enemies. Fighting for what is preferable, we can be tolerant while still rejecting the intolerable.

Umberto Eco 1994

♦ To forgive and forget we should know what actually happened.

Nelson Mandela on the Truth & Reconciliation Commission 1996

♦ Reconciliation . . . cannot be achieved unless there is also repentance on all sides . . . No single side in the conflict of the past has a monopoly of virtue or should bear responsibility for all the abuses that occurred. Nor can any side claim sole credit for the transformation of the country. The transformation belongs to us all.

FW De Klerk 1996

♦ It can never be easy. To me, really, it is just opening the wounds for nothing. Because these people are going to go to the Commission – I suppose they have applied or their names have been taken. But if they go there, are they going to tell the truth? Or are they going to lie so they will get amnesty?

Ntsiki Biko, widow of the murdered Black Consciousness leader Steve Biko 1996

UNITED NATIONS

UNIVERSAL DECLARATION OF HUMAN RIGHTS

URL

UNITED NATIONS

♦ The tragic situations in Palestine/Israel, Iraq and Bosnia are stark reminders that the UN has not lived up to its overblown Charter and Universal Declaration of Human Rights.

♦ The UN must cease to reflect the interests of those who run it so that it can practise what it preaches; otherwise, its noble sentiments could end up like those in the divine books: fine on paper and nothing else.

Abdullah al Udhari 1998

♦ The collective UN vision has always been in conflict with the practical self-interest of individual states, a dualism that has been strongly criticised even within the organisation.

Robert Maharaj 1994

♦ The UN is necessary to secure at least the humanitarian aid supply routes. Any other role for the UN would be meaningless – it simply does not have enough power to fulfil its mandate in Bosnia. Even if they had a different mandate, I doubt the situation would change. UN is trying not to be biased in this war. Every soldier, though, comes with a different opinion, some prejudices. When enough of the same prejudice gets accumulated, they are and must be biased.

Damir, Bosnian medical student 1995

♦ To me the United Nations was the supreme organisation, I had faith in it, the very word United Nations gave me faith. I do not know what has happened elsewhere, but here they have betrayed this trust. They contribute to the striving to divide our country.

Semsa on Bosnia 1995

♦ The UN thinks the Cyprus ceasefire, which has lasted 30 years, is a big success. As far as Boutros-Ghali is concerned, success is measured not by a final settlement but by the sole yardstick of keeping the guns silent. It would not have bothered them at all if we had all gone on talking for ten years.

♦ There was never a sense, in UN pronouncements, that it might be important to make a distinction between a just and an unjust peace.

David Rieff 1995

♦ Once states have imploded, someone must come in and administer the society on a day to day basis, until ordinary people can shake off the fear and loathing which divide them. This means rule by strangers. Yet such exercises are a potential incitement to insurrection unless they have the legitimacy of an international mandate. In other words, the next task facing the international community is to devise a form of trusteeship. However, the great powers are as reluctant to administer the peace as they were to end the war [in former Yugoslavia]. Everywhere, there is a retreat from obligation, a retreat covered by moral disgust. When conscience is the only linkage between rich and poor, North and South, zones of safety and zones of danger, it is a weak link indeed. The real impediment to sustained solidarity with Bosnia was some nearly incorrigible feeling that their fate and ours are severed: we may owe them our pity but we do not share their fate. The fact that ethnic civil war elsewhere prefigures what will happen at home if our states fail to hold the ring in our own multi-ethnic tensions was not enough to make people feel the Yugoslav cause to be their own. Most of us persist in the belief that while the fires far away are terrible things, we can keep them from our doors. Now they are in Europe itself, barely two hours from our homes. It is not our conscience alone which should connect us to these zones, but the most soberly egotistical calculation of our interest. This is the frontier of awareness we have to cross.

Michael Ignatieff 1995

♦ What are the guidelines by which the world is to order itself following the collapse of the geo-political model drawn up at Yalta? The UN was created as an integral part of that model. Do we now want to strengthen and equip it with effective means of action? Or is it to be a political International Red Cross which, though perhaps necessary, cannot promise people any kind of resolution?

Tadeusz Mazowiecki 1995

♦ In the past 50 years, all regimes practising human rights abuses have taken refuge behind the UN Charter's guarantees of state sovereignty and non-interference.

Michael Ignatieff 1998

UNIVERSAL DECLARATION OF HUMAN RIGHTS

♦ The hard basics of humanitarianism are still there in the great Conventions of 1948 and 1949. They are as valid as ever: an inspired and enduringly relevant combination of pragmatism and principle.

Alex de Waal 1998

♦ The Universal Declaration of Human Rights is a fine piece of aspirational rhetoric, but the governments that signed it never thought of it as binding.

Bill Orme 1998

♦ The Universal Declaration was built not upon trust in ourselves, but on fear.

Michael Ignatieff 1998

♦ The universality of rights has encouraged people everywhere to demand their rights; and has legitimised efforts by inter-governmental bodies, governments, non-governmental organisations and individuals elsewhere to protect the right of their fellow human beings, not only those of their fellow countrymen and women.

Aryeh Neier 1998

♦ Measured against the status of human rights in the world today, the Declaration's failures are more obvious than its successes. For those who have no experience of freedom, it's difficult to understand. Its principles need no expansion, but their effects should touch all people: it will have real impact only when everyone understands it, even the illiterate.

Martin Simecka 1998

♦ Having read – and signed – the Declaration is like having tasted the fruit from the tree of knowledge. There is, however, no angel with flaming sword to expel governments violating human rights from their Eden of national sovereignty.

Konstanty Gebert 1998

♦ I have my own wish list. But at the top is an end to hypocrisy.

Noam Chomsky 1998

♦ Count up the results of 50 years of human rights mechanisms, 30 years of multi-billion dollar development programmes and endless high level rhetoric and the global impact is quite underwhelming.

Mary Robinson 1998

♦ Any concept of human rights that is to be universally accepted and globally enforced demands equal respect and mutual comprehension between rival cultures.

♦ What is at issue – between those who support a universal concept and those who argue for a relativist approach – is how and by whom these rights are to be defined and articulated. Universality requires global agreement, a consensus between different societies and cultures, not the application of one set of standards derived from the culture and context of a particular society to all other societies.

Abdullahi An-Na'im 1994

♦ Without the Declaration, the history of the second half of the twentieth century would have been even crueller. In the 1980s, the human rights world was politicised.

Martin Simecka 1998

URL (UNIFORM RESOURCE LOCATOR)

♦ Would-be citizens of nations without a country to call their own are staking out their territory in cyberspace:

www.tibet.com	The Government of Tibet in Exile
www.boreale.se www.saamefolket.se	The Sami people, indigenous population of Scandinavia
www.klc.org.pk	The Government of Azad Jammu and Kashmir
www.krg.org	Kurdistan Regional Government

♦ www.ezln.org. The crisis in the southern Mexican state of Chiapas will not be solved in cyberspace, yet the internet can be a powerful tool for activism and information dissemination.

♦ www.taino-tribe.org/jatiboni.html. A website that provides a wide range of contacts for people interested in the Taino Native American Indian heritage of the Caribbean and Florida diaspora. An open internet forum helps promote awareness of and interest in the Jatibonicu Taino tribal nation's educational and cultural non-profit organisations.

♦ www.unpo.org. UNPO (Unrepresented Nations and Peoples Organisation) is an international organisation created by nations and peoples around the world who are not represented in the principal international organisations such as the United Nations. Founded in 1991, UNPO today consists of over 50 members who represent over 100 million people.

VIOLENCE

VIOLENCE

♦ The problem of domestic violence has no cultural or class boundaries. In Britain, it has only recently been recognised as an arena for state intervention. In many countries, where women continue to be defined as the property of their husbands, domestic violence is seen to be a private matter. In cultures as diverse as Sri Lanka and Kenya, there are folk sayings interpreting wife-beating as an act of love.

Naila Kabeer 1995

♦ Diasporic people often become stubbornly conservative and it is the women who are always blamed if the children get rebellious.

♦ Among the most deprived and easily threatened groups in this country, there is evidence of increasing oppression. Young girls, deeply loved as children, are imprisoned, beaten, starved by the men and the older women in the family, who fear being ostracised themselves. Many girls run away from home. Some are taken on 'holiday' and forced into marriages before they finish school. Others are recaptured after their education.

♦ It is fear that drives these parents to cruelty and things will only change when those who determine the values of a community – the religious leaders in particular – can tell older women that God will punish them if they torture their daughters and daughers-in-law, and that these cultures will only survive if young girls are made to feel happy within them.

Yasmin Alibhai-Brown 2000

♦ The Geneva Conventions outlawed rape in war. 'Women', it declared, 'shall be especially protected . . . against rape, enforced prostitution, or any form of indecent assault.' Yet women, in almost every modern conflict, are being raped, both because rape is seen as a legitimate spoil of war, and because deliberate violence directed at women, and designed to dehumanise them, has become a recognised component of military strategy.

Caroline Moorehead 1995

♦ Military coups, which happen often in Burma, are violent ways of changing situations and I do not want to encourage and to perpetuate this tradition of bringing about change through violence. Because I'm afraid that if we achieve democracy in this way we will never be able to get rid of the idea that you bring necessary change through violence. The very method would be threatening us all the time. Because there are always people who do not agree with democracy. And if we achieve it through violent means, there will be the hard core of those who have always been against the democracy movement who will think, 'It was through violence that they changed the system and if we can develop our own methods of violence which are superior to theirs, we can get back the power.' And we'll go on in this vicious cycle. for me it is as much a political tactic as a spiritual belief, that violence is not the right way.

Aung San Suu Kyi 1997

♦ With the disintegration of the socialist system throughout Eastern Europe, wife-beating is on the increase. But everyone conspires to keep the secret: women are ashamed to report it; and if they do, the authorities dismiss it as trivial.

♦ There is nowhere to go. The housing shortage, women's lack of economic independence, the fact that many couples have to live together during and after divorce, that there is no such thing as a restriction order and that it is up to the women to get out – all these contribute to the blanket of silence over domestic abuse. If the woman does leave home she forfeits the right to any share of the property when she divorces. And then there is the disapproval, the shame, the nagging emotional dependence, the loss of self-esteem, the fear. To resist, to speak and show signs of breaking out are the most dangerous things she can do. That is when killings happen.

Irena Maryniak on Hungary 2000

W

WAR

WHISTLEBLOWERS

WOMEN

WORDS

WRITERS

WAR

♦ War is always a bad time for free speech, because political and social pressures chill any genuine criticism of, or even debate about, governments' security and military measures.

Ronald Dworkin 2002

♦ The war in the Gulf [1990/91] marks a major change in censorship. Although the Alliance gives 'military security' as its ostensible reason for the rules it has imposed on correspondents – the excuse used ever since the British invented military censorship in 1856 – there has been a covert expansion of aims. In the Gulf War, the Alliance goal is much more ambitious – to manage the news to its own advantage.

♦ News management in the Gulf has three main purposes: to deny information to the enemy; to create and maintain support for the war; and to change public perception of the nature of war itself. Of these the third is by far the most important and the most sinister. How did we get to this alarming state of affairs?

♦ On 25 February 1856, British commander-in-chief Sir William Codrington issued a general order that must rank as the origin of military censorship. It forbade the publication of anything the authorities considered could be of value to the enemy.

♦ Britain has been involved in no major war since then in which some degree of censorship has not been imposed. And as early as the First World War, the government had expanded the aims of censorship to include point number two from above – create and maintain support for the war.

♦ In 1914–18, the military allowed only six correspondents to report from the front. It put them in officer's uniform, provided them with orderlies, lorries, cars, conducting officers and censors. The censors lived with them, ate with them, read their dispatches, and opened their private letters.

♦ The aims were to provide the public with colourful stories of heroism and glory so as to sustain enthusiasm for the war, to cover any mistakes the high command might make, preserve it from criticism in its conduct of the war, and to safeguard the reputations of the generals.

♦ By 1939, the government had come to regard the war correspondent as a part of the armed forces – 'an integral and essential part of our fighting activities on land, on the sea and in the air' – who, for the most part, again went along willingly with what the censors said. This was understandable because the war was one of national survival in which the wickedness of the enemy did not have to be invented.

♦ But it did produce worrying after-effects – when censorship was finally lifted many correspondents were bewildered. One spoke for them all when he said: 'But where will we go now to have our stories cleared?' A Canadian, Charles Lynch, summed up: 'It's humiliating to look back at what we wrote during the war. We were a propaganda arm of our governments. At the start the censors enforced that, but by the end we were our own censors. We were cheerleaders.'

♦ Vietnam upset the status quo . . . At first correspondents supported the war, but when they saw that government policy was not working they said so. Graphic television coverage brought home to Americans the nature of the war itself, its bloody brutality, and the suffering of Vietnamese civilians. That, and increasing American casualties, sapped public support for the war and the United States pulled out.

♦ Robin Day, then a BBC commentator, said that war on colour television screens in American living rooms had made Americans far more anti-militarist and anti-war than anything else. 'One wonders if in future a democracy which has uninhibited television coverage in every home will ever be able to fight a war, however just?'

♦ By the time the Falklands campaign had started, the [UK] Ministry of Defence (MoD) had in place its plan to manage the news . . . The MoD succeeded in managing the news brilliantly – censoring, suppressing, and delaying dangerous news, releasing bad news in dribs and drabs so as to nullify its impact, and projecting its own image as the only real source of accurate information about what was happening.

♦ A new language was brought into being to soften the reality of war. Bombing military targets in the heart of cities was called 'denying the enemy an infrastructure'. People were 'soft targets'. Saturation bombing was 'laying down a carpet'.

♦ So the Gulf War is an important one in the history of censorship. It marks a deliberate attempt by the authorities to alter public perception of the nature of war itself, particularly the fact that civilians die in war. The rationale, as yet unproven, is that the public will no longer support any war in which large numbers of civilians are killed, especially by Western high technology armaments. Whether the new censorship succeeds or not remains to be seen.

Phillip Knightley 1991

♦ On 11 December 1994, the Russian army invaded the Republic of Chechnya 'in order to restore constitutional order' and eliminate a regime of 'bandits and criminals'. According to the ex-minister of defence, Pavel Grachov, the operation was to last a few hours: a simple victory parade.

♦ In little more than a year and a half of conquest, the army has suffered greater losses than in the 12 years of its disastrous adventure in Afghanistan. Hence the pathetic efforts of state television and press to conceal the wretched truth, to cover up the barbarism, clumsiness and disorganisation of military operations, transmuting disasters into heroic actions, rehearsing the ritual litany of the ' imminent liquidation of the last bandit hide-outs'. Despite so much fabrication and self-deception – a legacy of the defunct regime of the USSR – Shamil Basayev's incursions in Budennovsk and Raduyev's in Kiliar with the victorious return of both to Chechnya in the face of intense army fire that inflicted more losses in their own ranks than in the enemy's, opened the eyes of a sector of public opinion and upped the number of citizens opposed to the war.

♦ To conceal the magnitude of the urbicide, mountains of debris were heaped up and thrown on the rubbish tips and pits around Grozny. The infill work proceeds and the authors of the 'feat' have cast a veil of metal fences around the affected area to ward off prying eyes.

Juan Goytisolo 1996

♦ Euphemism is the subtlest form of censorship, and the Gulf War has been a riot of euphemism. The crisis rapidly generated its own lexicon, a language with its origins in military jargon, which has mediated between the battlefield and the public and provided a form of psychological insulation from the bitter reality of war.

♦ Never have so many synonyms for 'to kill' or 'to destroy' been assembled outside the pages of a thesaurus: to 'degrade', to 'interdict', to 'stealth', to 'take out', to 'impact', to 'suppress', to 'eliminate', to 'decapitate', to 'de-air', to 'down' or to 'neutralise' have all been used.

Khafji was said to be 'cleansed' after the removal of Iraqi troops. General Colin Powell was more up-front in his promise that when the Allied forces came up against the Iraqi army they would 'cut it off and kill it', the image of amputation echoing the equally medical idea of 'surgical bombing'.

♦ However surgical the AAF (Allied Air Forces) have tried to be, 'circular error probability' (the circle around a target within which a weapon is likely to fall) remains a problem. Civilian casualties unlucky enough to find themselves in a 'target-rich environment' fall under the heading of 'collateral damage', which – according to BDAs (Bomb Damage Assessments), to which the Allied Command attached a 'high confidence value' – is almost invariably 'minimal'; since mid-February, the more candid 'civilian impacting' has also enjoyed a vogue at the briefing lectern. The collective noun for the aircraft doing the damage is 'package' (as in a 'package' of aeroplanes), although, confusingly, 'package' is also used to refer to a targeting campaign. Ensuring that aircraft on the same side don't crash into one another is a matter of 'deconfliction'.

♦ Rarely has it been so obvious that language is volatile stuff, that it succumbs easily to manipulation, to the sedulous distortions of propagandists and censors. In the Gulf War, words have been used to salve the conscience, to cordon off the truth, rather than to communicate it.

Matthew D'Ancona 1991

♦ The greatest bravery a war correspondent can show is to report differently at a time when news conformity is the norm.

Mark Pedelty 2002

♦ The most significant legacy of war is that it legitimises violence as a form of political activity.

Alex de Waal 1999

WAR REPORTING

Jake Lynch

The provisions of the BBC's Royal Charter are handed down to journalists on tablets of stone known as Producers' Guidelines. Here's what they have to say about reporting in wartime: 'All views should be reflected in due proportion to mirror the depth and spread of opinion in the United Kingdom.'

It contains an unacknowledged myth: that news – or at least BBC news – holds up a mirror to the world from which we can retrieve a full picture of reality as it happened. In practice, the reflection we see is distorted by conventions and biases that amount to pervasive self-censorship.

As Robert Fisk points out in the *Independent*, one sure sign that the US is preparing for military action is when newspaper front pages become a daily 'notice board' for 'sources' from within the administration.

They brief journalists anonymously to float ideas and soften up the public for war. Many such stories start life with Associated Press, the venerable US news agency that serves more than 5,000 publications across the country. AP has its own guidelines: a 'style book' of dos and don'ts for its reporters in the field. One of its stipulations is that once a source has spoken, even 'on condition of anonymity', that's a story. And, as anyone who's ever worked for a news agency knows, once you've got a story you move it or the world moves on.

AP journalists, like most others, work with a rough-and-ready, practical version of the 'mirror' theory of news: 'we just report the facts'. But it is the reporting convention itself that provides the opportunity for 'facts' to be created. It's journalists' willingness to pass uncritically into the public realm claims that Iraq is linked to al-Qaida or that the Pentagon is already drawing up plans for a lightning strike on Baghdad, merely on the say-so of an unnamed source, that encourages the next source to feed them another titbit from the top table. Cumulatively, this determines not only the way their public read the news, but constructs in advance its reaction to the translation of 'facts' into actual events.

Inevitably, there comes a time in any campaign to go on the record. And this is where another reporting convention becomes influential. I'm talking about the enduring primacy of 'official' information. Ben Bagdikian, former *Washington Post* editor, has educated thousands of readers in the origins of this convention – the commercial imperative in US newspapers to be all-things-to-all-people in their own town or city and thus drive out competitors.

Bagdikian calls it the convention of 'objectivity', a way of appearing to remove partisanship from the news. Hence, for instance, the reason why a speech by Tony Blair is reported is not because we agree with what he has to say, but because he's the Prime Minister. This convention also has a visible influence on the behaviour of our sources. As when Blair used his speech to the Trades Union Congress in September 2002 to issue a warning that, without attending to the 'threat' from Iraq, it would some day 'engulf us'. A formulation of studied vagueness and a way of ringing alarm bells without having to spell out a plausible scenario or sequence of events that posed a danger only military action could forestall.

But these omissions would have passed unnoticed by any but the most vigilant members of the public. The speech was reported 'straight' – at least on TV, which is where most people get news. You don't, when reporting a major set-piece speech by the PM, assemble a 'supporting cast' to pick holes in it. That's the convention, something Downing Street would know perfectly well when planning the speech and its message.

Now consider the other side of this coin: if the conventions dictate what goes in, what gets left out? Here's where self-censorship is most visible. The Pew Research Centre, in one of its mammoth global opinion polls, found that nearly half of all Britons – 44% – believe any attack on Iraq would have nothing to do with any threat from weapons of mass destruction: it's the oil. That view was shared by 54% of Germans, 75% of French and substantial majorities in most other countries.

A Channel 4 poll presented respondents in Britain with a menu of options on what they believed was really at stake. Dealing with Saddam's threat to world peace – the official version – came top with 22%, but grabbing Iraqi oil was just one percentage point behind.

Has BBC output 'reflected' the 'depth and spread of opinion in the UK' as it is mandated to do? Hardly. Neither is the picture any different in the press. War-drums started to beat in earnest with Bush's 'state of the Union' address to Congress on 30 January 2002 where he coined the phrase 'Axis of Evil' for Iraq, Iran and North Korea.

Of almost 9,000 articles in the UK press between then and mid-December that contained the words 'Iraq', 'Saddam' and 'weapons', only about 180 paid the slightest attention to oil as a motivating factor – except to dismiss it as fanciful. A large proportion of these was accounted for by readers' letters.

Tony Blair's 'engulf us' formulation was choreographed with a parallel attempt by George Bush, to convince Americans that Iraq posed a clear and present danger to them. The threat to the US, he declared, was 'great and growing'. But opinion polls suggest the respective publics of the two countries remain unconvinced. So the case for war has fallen back on the tried and trusted formula of ensuring 'regional security'.

What is striking is how rarely journalists ask any other country in the region: 'What is your assessment of the Iraqi threat and how would you deal with it?' Instead, the story is usually framed as though it were designed for a cover of *Newsweek*, like that of early October 2002 where twin images of Presidents Bush and Saddam faced off over the words 'who will win?'

The framing and the question go hand in hand. This is conflict-as-game: two players, one ball. Any development begs to be analysed only in so far as it moves us closer to victory for one or the other. Each 'player' faces only two alternatives: victory or defeat. And since defeat is unthinkable, each steps up his efforts for victory. Framing a conflict in this way is inherently escalatory.

The 'mirror' theory of news is a way of disavowing responsibility for any of this. But it is increasingly visible, both to journalists and their audiences, that it is not the full story. What is needed is an ethical framework or 'checklist' that can serve as an antidote to the stranglehold of conventions, a dangerous form of self-censorship.

Crucially, any checklist must also offer a set of criteria for audiences to help them assess the ethical content of international reporting and demand a better deal from journalists. A formula for challenging censorship and self-censorship in favour of the news we need in this interdependent world.

www.reportingtheworld.org

WHISTLEBLOWERS

♦ Reactions to whistleblowers – whether they act anonymously or speak out openly – are often ambivalent. The person we consider has performed a heroic public service will, in other eyes, be betraying the trust of colleagues or the institution. Blowing the whistle may sometimes be the wrong thing to do; but when something is seriously wrong, when the public is put at risk, and when a conscientious employee has tried everything to remedy the matter from the inside, the issues become clearer. The overriding public interest may lie in protecting our right to be told, and the whistleblower's right not to be punished for telling us.

♦ The contracts of both public and private sector employees [recently institutions] increasingly contain gagging clauses, making the unauthorised disclosure of any information to anyone a disciplinary offence that could lead to dismissal.

♦ The victims of unfair dismissal, sex discrimination or dangerous consumer products may get their compensation – but only in return for a binding promise of silence.

♦ Could whistleblowing ever be rendered unnecessary? A powerful Freedom of Information Act – which would expose information without the need for leaking – would help, but could never be more than a partial solution.

Maurice Frankel on the UK 1995

♦ When Mordechai Vanunu wrote, 'Don't look at the whole machine . . . Don't concern yourself with things beyond your grasp,' he invited us to realise that imagination would make that impossible. Vanunu, working at Dimona on the then secret Israeli nuclear bomb programme, found he could no longer separate his actions from their consequence, the weapon from its effects. He had to speak.

♦ On 30 September 1986, five days before his revelations were made public, Vanunu was kidnapped and taken back to Israel.

AL Kennedy 2002

WOMEN

♦ A few years ago, around 30 Western-educated women drove their cars publicly through the streets of Riyadh, in direct challenge to the ban on women drivers. They were arrested, thrown out of their jobs and considered 'prostitutes' by some clergymen.

Abdul Bari-Atwan on Saudi Arabia 1996

♦ At the present rate of female foetal abortion in China, there will be 70 million men condemned to celibacy by the year 2000.

Jesse Banfield 1997

♦ There is no group in the world more censored by the sin of omission than widows.

♦ What all widows share, wherever they are from, is the fact that there are far more of them than widowers.

♦ For many widows throughout Asia and Africa the death of a husband spells poverty, instant and crushing.

Caroline Moorehead 1998

♦ We should not be surprised when women, however conservatively, place a greater value on the traditions of their own culture than on personal freedom, since for each of us personal identity is so deeply bound up with culture. There are undoubtedly women (and men) who would rather that such difficult issues were not discussed. Yet it is precisely this aspect of censorship that itself requires discussion.

♦ Caught between the anything-goes amorality of consumer culture and the legacy of a repressive past, women have a difficult balance to maintain. The 'pornography wars' of the 1980s exemplified these difficulties.

Elizabeth Wilson 2000

♦ The denial that women have anything important to say is inherent in some editors' viewpoints – sexism, I am sure, they would not recognise.

♦ This is not 'intentional' censorship – but it can be worse than the orthodox form since it operates just as surely – but invisibly – to stop ideas from reaching others. It is not glorified by the noble martyrdom attached to the word 'censorship'. We are talking about the media. Media distortion, harassment, character assassination and disinformation [about women] is another form of censorship and can be almost worse than being ignored by editors and reviewers.

Shere Hite 1994

♦ From the uncompromising feminist academics such as Catherine MacKinnon, whose influential book *Only Words* argues that words themselves are the very agency of inequality, racial and sexual harassment, and sexual offences against women and children, to the doughty old Christian campaigner, Mary Whitehouse, who tried to keep explicit sex off TV screens in Britain, women of left and right have proved themselves sisters under the skin in calling for, and upholding, forms of censorship.

Mary Kenny 2000

♦ As women's rights activists have argued forcefully, large areas of human rights violations are not perceived, or not acted on, either by the development community or the human rights agencies because they occur in the domestic/cultural realm which the official human rights agenda does not encompass. They also entail the body of the economic agent in a way that does not fall within the purview of development planning. Yet these violations are indivisible dimensions of the more visible economic inequalities that have found a legitimate place on the development agenda: in health, education, as members of the labour force and political participation.

♦ If there is one common factor in the way that gender inequality is maintained in different cultures, it is in the reduction of women to their bodies and the simultaneous construction of their bodies and, hence, of women themselves, as inferior.

Naila Kabeer 1995

♦ If they have education, women have independence, they can feed themselves with their own earnings.

Rizia Begum 1998

♦ Most of the world's refugees and casualties of war are women and children. And as repressive governments are discovering, women make excellent targets, to be killed, raped, ill-treated or taken hostage in order to humiliate and inflict pain on them, and because it brings pressure on their husbands and families.

♦ Nowhere are the rights of women more comprehensively violated than by the legal process; no country treats its women as well as its men.

♦ According to a recent report put out by UNICEF, over a million newborn girls are murdered or left to die every year – simply because they are born females.

Caroline Moorehead 1995

♦ A woman is 10 times more likely to be raped than to die in a car crash.

♦ A woman over 65 has a 60% greater chance of living in poverty than a man of the same age.

♦ Black women are nearly four times as likely to be murdered as white women.

♦ A woman is battered every 15 seconds.

♦ Twenty-one per cent of married women report physical abuse by their husbands

Statistics compiled by Laura Bruni and Nevine Mabro 1995

♦ According to estimates from the International Organisation for Migration, as many as half a million women [sex workers] are brought every year from Eastern and Central Europe into the European Union. The majority are aged between 18 and 25, but increasing numbers are younger. Some are transported by force, some are aware they are coming to sell themselves, but most are duped.

Alan Hope 2000

WORDS

♦ Words matter. In a country that has always had elements of paranoia in its politics, and more so now than for years, it is foolish to dismiss the strident rhetoric of the airwaves and of politics as without influence.

Anthony Lewis on the US 1995

♦   The word bites like a fish.
        Shall I throw it back free
        Arrowing to that sea
        Where thoughts lash tail and fin?
        Or shall I pull it in
        To rhyme upon a dish?

Stephen Spender 1995

♦ Extermination plan: strip the land of grass, root up the last living plant, cover the earth with salt. After that, erase the memory of grass. To colonise consciousness, suppress it; to suppress it, empty it of past. Wipe out any sign that there was anything in this land other than silence, prisons and graves.

♦ Remembering is prohibited.

♦ There are customs regulations for words, incinerators for words, cemeteries for words.

♦ Squads of prisoners are sent out at night to cover with white paint the words of protest which in other times covered the walls of the city.

♦ The rain's persistent washing begins to dissolve the white paint. And there appear, gradually, the stubborn words.

Eduardo Galeano on Uruguay 1978

♦ Another thing, perhaps even more important: one of the expressions of the various obsessive neuroses which I suffered from at that time (or perhaps still do) is one that is well known to every dissident: you live in fear for your manuscript. Until such a time as the text which means so much to you is safely stowed somewhere, or distributed in several copies among other people, you live in a state of constant suspense and uncertainty – and as the years go by, surprisingly enough, this does not get easier but, on the contrary, the fear tends to grow into a pathological obsession. And if, at first, all you feared was a police search of your house or person, so that you hid your manuscript with friends every night, in time this fear becomes far more universal – you begin to worry that they'll lock you up tomorrow, that you'll fall ill or die, that something indefinite is going to happen to you (and the more indefinite the danger you fear, the more advanced is your disease), all this making it impossible for your work to see the light of day. As that work grows in size, your suspense grows in keeping with it – what if someone will trip you just as you are approaching the tape? You can't imagine how

I always looked forward to the time when I would have no work in progress! And prison only served to increase these fears.

Václav Havel 1986

♦ Power, while seeming to fuse with words through the process of their multiplication and distribution, eventually causes words themselves to become unfree.

Goenawan Mohamad 1997

♦ Censors bear witness to the power of the word even more forcefully than writers and readers, because they acknowledge in their fear the possibility of social and individual transformation running through the weave of stories.

Alberto Manguel and Craig Stephenson 1996

♦ The language of death: euphemisms that kill:

Cirugía (surgery): a form of killing whereby a victim's stomach is cut open, filled with stones and sewn up.

Corte de corbata (necktie cut): the victim is beheaded, his tongue is cut off and then placed on the torso to resemble a tie.

Donación (donation): money paid as a result of extortion or in exchange for hostages.

Fumigar (to fumigate): to kill, systematically and indiscriminately, real or supposed opponents.

Limpiar (to clean): to kill systematically or indiscriminately.

Llevar la lápida al cuello (to wear a headstone around one's neck): to risk being killed following death threats.

Marcar calavera (to look like a skeleton): to be very close to death or on a death list.

Sufragio (suffrage): condolences sent to the victim, indicating the day and hour of his or her execution.

Amanda Romero on Colombia 2000

WRITERS

♦ The opposite of censorship is self-expression, which we call literature.

Stephen Spender 1994

♦ The case files I have studied are tightly interwoven with our own lives. Many of these writers are working far harder now than contemporary authors. They have a deeper effect on the consciousness of the readership. We found extracts of a novel by Platonov in the Lubianka. No one knew it was there, not even Platonov's daughter. It's a work which is highly relevant today. Even the word *perestroika* features . . . A 'great' writer is a rarity after all. But I've come across some very significant ones. There are a number of manuscripts of the calibre of Evgenia Ginzburg's *Journey into the Whirlwind*. But we have only just begun. And you can't quantify literary discoveries. Anything may turn up. We have found an unknown novel by Platonov and discovered Kluyev's best poetry. For now, those two names vindicate the effort and the struggle.

♦ We met with resistance, of course: a kind of elastic wall which gave a little and then sent us right back to where we had started. There are officials who have no interest in seeing the material made public. Many were involved in the cases I examined; writers frequently informed on their colleagues. Some are still living, and very comfortably too. They are scarcely enthusiastic about our work. This isn't just an academic project; it's explosive material. The KGB archives are a dossier on everybody. Anyone can be exposed. And there were many, many thousands of informers. The victims died. Those who denounced them are still with us.

Vitaly Shentalinsky on the USSR 1991

♦ Soviet renegades manipulated by Western forces became a weapon of Western ideology and propaganda. Works which were insignificant from the aesthetic point of view were praised to the skies. Criticism was forbidden.

♦ By the early 1990s, the Cold War was over and Soviet communism defeated. Soviet political leaders performed an ideological volte-face, and thousands of writers and journalists followed their example.

Alexandr Zinovev 1996

♦ Under a communist regime, any author with the right contacts could expect, in due course, to see publication of a collected edition of his writings. No connection existed between production expenses and sales.

Irena Maryniak 1996

♦ For those of us who write books, it sometimes seems that it's open season on writers around the world nowadays, a horrifying state of affairs which this indispensable magazine [*Index on Censorship*] does so much to record and to protest against.

♦ It is perhaps the low-tech nature of the act of writing that will save it.

♦ What one writer can make in the solitude of one room is something no power can easily destroy. But beware the writer who sets himself or herself up as the voice of a nation.

Salman Rushdie 1996 and 1997

♦ Yes, it is a rotten position to be in. But if you have the courage to write something, then you have to have the courage to stick up for it.

♦ It is disgusting, of course, since the writer finds himself in a weird trap: he has a concept of life, he has a background and an upbringing and a point of view and his own ideas about life, all of which are what started him writing in the first place. But the situation develops in such a way that he finds himself forced to occupy himself with completely different activities. It is stupid and degrading; in my opinion it is a complete nonsense when the writer is forced to become a political activist.

Joseph Brodsky 1972

♦ We avenge the censorship we face in reality through our writing.

Satyavathi, Indian woman writer, 2002

♦ What is a writer's freedom?

To me it is his right to maintain and publish to the world a deep, intense, private view of the situation in which he finds his society. If he is to work as well as he can, he must take, and be granted, freedom from the public conformity of political interpretation, morals and tastes.

♦ Living when we do, where we do, as we do, 'freedom' leaps to mind as a political concept exclusively – and when people think of freedom for writers they visualise at once the great mound of burnt, banned and proscribed books our civilisation has piled up; a pyre to which our own country has added and is adding its contribution. The right to be left alone to write what one pleases is not an academic issue to those of use who live and work in South Africa.

♦ All that the writer can do, as a writer, is to go on writing the *truth as he sees it*. That is what I mean by his 'private view' of events, whether they be the great public ones of wars and revolutions, or the individual and intimate ones of daily, personal life.

♦ Bannings and banishments are terrible known hazards a writer must face, and many have faced, if the writer belongs where freedom of expression, among other freedoms, is withheld, but sometimes creativity is frozen rather than destroyed.

♦ A Thomas Mann survives exile to write a *Dr Faustus*; a Pasternak smuggles *Dr Zhivago* out of a ten-year silence; a Solzhenitsyn emerges with his terrible world intact in the map of *The Gulag Archipelago*. Nearer our home continent: a Chinua Achebe, writing from America, does not trim his prose to please a Nigerian regime under which he cannot live; a Dennis Brown grows in reputation abroad while his poetry remains forbidden at home; and a Breyten Breytenbach, after accepting the special dispensation from racialist law which allowed him to visit his home country with a wife who is not white, no doubt has to accept the equally curious circumstance that his publisher would not publish the book he was to write about the visit, since it was sure to be banned.

♦ The fact is, even on the side of the angels, a writer has to reserve the right to tell the truth as he sees it, in his own words, without being accused of letting the side down. For as Philip Toynbee has written, 'the writer's gift to the reader is not social zest or moral improvement or love of country, but an enlargement of the reader's apprehension'. This is the writer's unique contribution to social change. He needs to be left alone, by brothers as well as enemies, to make this gift. And he must make it even against his own inclination. I need hardly add this does not mean he retreats to an ivory tower. The gift cannot be made from any such place. The other day, Jean-Paul Sartre gave the following definition of the writer's responsibility to his society as an intellectual, after himself having occupied such a position in France for the best part of 70 years: 'He is someone who is faithful to a political and social body but never stops contesting it. Of course, a contradiction may arise between his fidelity and his *contestation*, but that's a fruitful contradiction. If there's fidelity without *contestation*, that's no good: one is no longer a free man.'

♦ Turgenev sums up: 'The life that surrounds him [the writer] provides him with the content of his works; he is its concentrated reflection; but he is as incapable of writing a panegyric as a lampoon . . . When all is said and done – that is beneath him. Only those who can do no better submit to a given theme or carry out a programme.'

Nadine Gordimer 1976

♦ And I know a little about the inviting temptation to simply get out at any cost, to quit my country in disgust and disillusion, as no small number of people did in the McCarthy 1950s and as a long line of Czechs and Slovaks have in these recent years. I also know the empty feeling in the belly at the prospect of trying to learn another nation's secret language, its gestures and body communications without which a writer is only half-seeing and half-hearing. So those who have chosen to remain as writers on their native soil despite remorseless pressure to emigrate are, perhaps no less than their oppressors, rather strange and anachronistic figures in this time.

♦ The oddest request I ever heard in Czechoslovakia – or anywhere else – was to do what I could to help writers publish their works – but not in French, German or English, the normal desire of sequestered writers cut off from the outside. No, these Czech writers were desperate to see their works – in Czech! Somehow this speaks of something far more profound than 'dissidence' or any political quantification. There is something like love in it, and in this sense it is a prophetic yearning and demand.

Arthur Miller 1978

♦ Exile compels the writer to become 'hot'. Leaving a society and readers makes writing lose all its practical significance.

♦ Writing that has no readers and has no audience is not necessarily a bad thing.

Gao Xingjian 2002

♦ This 'individualisation', this 'subjectification' is an enormous gain from a life of exile. I'm even prepared to tell friends that it's an essential process that takes away the necessities of social superficialities and replaces them with the individual's own internal necessities.

♦ That poem was like a long-distance journey through language, and it's only when you come back that your realise what you've gained from it.

Yang Lian 2002

♦
    The millstones of my thoughts can hardly turn,
        Too rare the flicker of light in my aching soul.
    Yes, tight is the circle around us tautly drawn,
        But my verses will burst their bonds and freely roam
    And I can guard, perhaps, beyond their reach,
        In rhythmic harmony this hard-won gift of speech.

Alexander Solzhenitsyn 1972, trans. Michael Scammell

♦ At the height of Stalin's dictatorship, Boris Pasternak was invited to an official writers' conference in Moscow. Pasternak knew that if he attended and spoke, he would be arrested for what he would say; if he attended and didn't speak, he would be arrested for contempt; if he didn't attend, he'd be arrested for disobeying the Dictator's invitation. Pasternak attended. The conference lasted three days. During the first day Pasternak said nothing. His friends begged him to speak, since he would be arrested anyway, and urged him to profit at least from the presence of an audience. Pasternak remained silent. He also remained silent on the second day. On the third day, however, he rose to his feet. The audience held its breath. At last, Pasternak opened his mouth and said, 'Thirty-two.' And the audience, recognising that he meant Shakespeare's thirty-second sonnet which Pasternak had brilliantly translated, roared out the words they knew by heart, and which across three centuries Pasternak had transformed into a promise of hope addressed to the reader, far beyond the will of Stalin:

> If thou survive my well-contented day
> When that churl Death my bones with dust shall cover . . .

Alberto Manguel and Craig Stephenson 1996

♦ Fiction gives dignity. It offers what no other form completely can – the articulated potential, the spoken dreams, the unmistakable beauty and the possibilities of the immense, human interior reality inside that Other.

♦ Fiction written by living authors who are oppressed, imprisoned or under threat – whatever its subject – screams that these authors are human, that any action taken to damage something so precious is irrevocably criminal.

♦ Any author, writing any kind of fiction on any topic, resists the forces that deny our common humanity.

AL Kennedy 2002

XENOPHOBIA

XINGXING

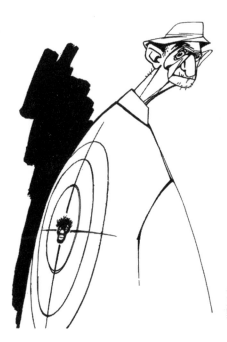

XENOPHOBIA

♦ What those who oppose US military action dislike about the atmosphere since 11 September is the oppressive moralism, the coercive appeals to patriotism, the rights violations of detainees, the renewed xenophobia and the general chill on free speech.

Michael Ignatieff 2002

♦ Racism and xenophobia work perfectly well without foreigners, for they are based on fear rather than on reality.

Elfriede Jelinek 2000

♦ The tabloids never really miss a chance to mock the French or the Germans; sometimes, it seems that the only two European peoples for whom the English have any time are the Dutch and the Russians. But exposure to continental European competition did the British economy a world of good. We would probably never have changed our ways had it not been for the competition from Europe, or the attractiveness of that vast market. And yet ignorance, or hostility, are the most common English reactions. Why?

Norman Stone 2001

XINGXING

♦ Xingxing (Stars) was a Chinese fine arts group formed in 1979. They were closely associated with the short-lived Democracy Wall movement. In the summer of 1979, the Xingxing artists held an unofficial modernist exhibition in a park which bordered the Beijing Art Gallery. The exhibition consisted of around 30 sculptures and 150 paintings which were hung from the park railings. Its opening day brought a large number of visitors.

The park authorities however were not so keen on the exhibition and the police became involved. They demanded that the exhibits were removed and returned the following day with police reinforcement to confiscate the artwork. They later returned the exhibits and promised a legal exhibition at a later date.

The Xingxing sent a petition to the Beijing authorities demanding the right to stage the exhibition. If they didn't receive a response, a rally would be held opposing the ban. No response was heard and the demonstrations took place on 1 October, coinciding with the 30th anniversary of the People's Republic of China. Very few of the Xingxing actually attended the demonstration because they were concerned that the authorities would reverse their decision on staging the exhibition.

On 20 November 1979, the authorities announced that Xingxing could hold their exhibition on the conditions that no advertisements would be carried in the press and that a number of sexually explicit sculptures were removed. Despite the lack of advertising, the exhibition gained crowds of around 7,000 visitors per day.

It wasn't until March 1980 that the first official publication *Meishu* (Fine Art) contained a positive review of the Xingxing.

Desmond A Skee, *Censorship: A World Encyclopaedia*

Hunt Emerson, 'AB seize it' from *Obscene*. Courtesy Knockabout Comics

YOUR POCKET GUIDE TO SEX

YFORUM.COM

YFORUM

♦ Y? – The National Forum On People's Differences – is a website designed to provide an anonymous forum for human beings of all kinds to talk openly, to examine their prejudices, their misconceptions, their phobias and their curiosities within the protective anonymity of cyberspace. 'Here you'll find a virtual database of differences – categorised and searchable. Most surprising about the content of Y? is how thoughtful and well considered some of the responses are to even the most demeaning questions. A kind of frank, sobering and occasionally intense discourse that tells more about who we are and how we feel about each other than you're likely to learn from a dozen sociology texts.'

www.yforum.com

YOUR POCKET GUIDE TO SEX

♦ *Your Pocket Guide to Sex* was a sex-education manual commissioned by the British Health Education Authority (HEA) in 1994. A survey carried out by 22,000 young people revealed that they looked to their friends and the media for advice rather than their parents. The book, written by Nick Fisher, an 'agony uncle', was aimed at 16–25 year olds, a group generally targeted for sex education in schools.

It was due to be published in March 1994. However, a minister of state at the Department of Health, Brian Mawhinney, disapproved of its content. The book was labelled 'inappropriate, distasteful and smutty'. The HEA backed him and withdrew the book, claiming that they had also had reservations concerning the language used in the book. As well as the language, it was criticised for failing to put sex into the context of a long-term relationship.

Your Pocket Guide to Sex was eventually published by Penguin Books in June 1994. The front cover included the statement: 'The book the government tried to ban.'

Martin Cloonan 2001

Z

Z
ZMAG/ZNET

Z

♦ The security forces confront a different challenge now after several hundred thousand Berbers descended on Algiers in mid-June to protest against police brutality and demand that Tamazight, the Berber language, be officially recognised. Four people died and 1,000 were injured in clashes that pitted rural Berbers, wearing the Tamazight symbol for 'Z' on their green and yellow shirts, against the majority Arab-speaking Algérois.

Michael Griffin 2001

ZMAG/ZNET

♦ *Zmag* (founded in 1988) is an independent US monthly of critical thinking on political, cultural, social and economic life in the US, available in print and online. Founded in 1995 and used by a quarter of a million people a week, Znet offers information not found in the mainstream through diverse watch areas and subsites, translations, archives, links to other progressive sites and a daily comment section.

www.zmag.org

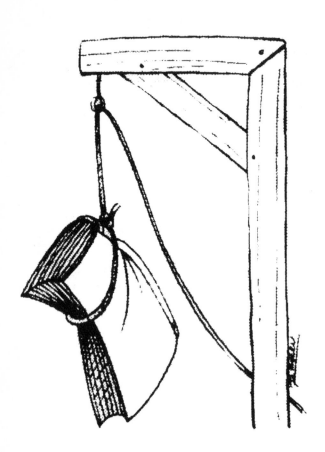

Sources

ACADEMIC FREEDOM
Abdol Karim Soroush *Squeeze on Democracy 1/2002*
Hilary and Steven Rose, Patrick Bateson *Varieties of Death 4/2002*

ACCESS TO INFORMATION
Salman Rushdie *Publishing Now 2/1996*
John Mortimer *September 1988*

ADVERTISING
Dan Schiller *The Future 3/1997*
Candelaria van Strien-Reney *Censorship: a World Encyclopaedia*
   (Fitzroy Dearborn, UK 2001)

ANTI-SEMITISM
Jean-Paul Sartre 1955, quoted by Nicholas Fraser *Race Matters July 2001*
Rafal Pankowski *Women Who Censor 2002*

ARMS
Anthony Sampson *November/December 1991*

ART
Roger Kimball *Art Unleashed 3/1996*
Edward Lucie-Smith *The Future 3/1997*
Elizabeth Wilson *Women Who Censor 2/2000*

ASYLUM
Nicholas Fraser *Race Matters 3/2001*
Jeremy Harding *Manufacturing Monsters 5/2000*

BANNING
Alberto Manguel *Publishing Now 2/1996*
Nicholas Fraser *Race Matters 3/2001*

Alberto Manguel *Gay's the Word in Moscow 1/1995*
Erica Jong *The Body Politic 4/1995*
Gill Newsham *Filling the Silence 2/2002*
Paul Oppenheimer *Hate Speech 1/1998*
Tariq Ali *The Silence of Madness 2/2001*

BLASPHEMY

Stephen's Digest of the Criminal Law, 9th edition 1950
David Nash *Censorship: A World Encyclopaedia 2002*
Ronald Dworkin *Rewriting History 3/1995*

BODIES

Judith Levine *Women Who Censor 2/2000*
Naila Kabeer *The Body Politic 4/1995*
Mary Kenny *Varieties of Death 4/2002*
Kim Normanton, Stembiso *Women Who Censor 2/2000*

BOOKS

Alberto Manguel, Margaret Atwood *Word Power 2/1999*
Urvashi Butalia *Publishing Now 2/1996*

BOOK BURNING

Italo Calvino *Lost Words 6/1996*
Fiction, Fact and the Fatwa: A Chronology of Censorship (Article 19, 1992)
Ray Bradbury *Word Power 2/1999*
Eduardo Galeano *March/April 1978*
Mary Kenny *Manufacturing Monsters 5/2000*

CAPITAL PUNISHMENT

Caroline Moorehead, Christopher Hitchens, Gov. William F Weld,
    Hugo Bedau, Richard Dieter, Michael L Radelet *March/April 1995*

CENSORSHIP

Alberto Manguel *1/1995*
Amy Adler *Art Unleashed 3/1996*
Ronald Dworkin, Harvey J Kaye *Rewriting History 3/1995*

Arthur C Clarke *The Subversive Eye 6/1995*
Anneliese Rohrer *Race Matters 3/2001*
Ivan Klíma *Post-Wall World November/December 1994*
Jesse Banfield *The Future 3/1997*
Susan Sontag *Squeeze on Democracy 1/2002*
Jack Mapanje, Michael Schmidt *Banned Poetry 5/1997*
Eduardo Galeano *March/April 1978*
Salman Rushdie *December 1983*
Jerzy Popieuszko *February 1985*
Martin Baker *August 1985*
Meir Vanunu *10/1991*
AL Kennedy, Hindi writer, Anamika, Ritu Menon *Filling the Silence 2/2002*
Gregory Palast *Big Science 3/1999*

CHILDREN
Irena Maryniak, Caroline Moorehead, Carol Bellamy *Looking at Kids 2/1997*
Nadine Strossen *September/October 1995*
Eduardo Galeano *March/April 1978*
Adewale Maja-Pearce *Rewriting History 3/1995*

CORRUPTION
He Qinglian on China *Filling the Silence 2/2002*
Anon *The Full Cover Up 5/1998*

DEATH
Mumia Abu-Jamal, Christopher Hitchens *Liberty in Britain 2/1995*
Aminatta Forna, AC Grayling *Varieties of Death 4/2002*

DEMOCRACY
Darryl Pinckney *God is Not Dead 4/1996*
Leonardo Boff *The Last Empire 1/1999*
Vladimir Bukovsky *The Silence of Madness 4/2001*
Nicholas Fraser *Race Matters 3/2001*
Irena Maryniak, Adam Michnik *Post-Wall World November/December 1994*
Nadine Gordimer on South Africa *July/August 1994*
John Keane *Squeeze on Democracy 1/2002*

Michael Ignatieff *Filling the Silence 2/2002*
Ernesto Sábato *1986* see also *Filling the Silence 2/2002*

DIASPORAS

Tom Cheesman and Marie Gillespie, Akash Kapur, Salil Tripathi
  Diaspora Voices 3/2002
Mrs Cheng *The Privacy Issue 3/2000*

DICTATORSHIP

Eduardo Galeano on Uruguay *March/April 1978*
Vera Rich *Secret Chernobyls 1/1996*
George Mangakis, Anon *Spring/1972*
Adam Michnik *Hate Speech 1/1998*

DISAPPEARED

Juan Goytisolo, Alberto Manguel *Wounded Nations Broken Lives 5/1996*
Michael Young *The New Slavery 1/2000*
Ernesto Sábato (1986) *Filling the Silence 2/2002*

DISSENT

John Mortimer *September 1988*
Dusan Reljic *After the Fall 5/1999*
Simon Kuper *This Sporting Life 4/2000*
Josh Passell *UN: Make or Break 5/1995*
Václav Havel *September/October 1979*

EDUCATION

Naila Kabeer, Sufia Begum, Zahera Khatoon *Gagged for It 3/1998*

ENVIRONMENT

Andrew Wasley, Marites Vitug, Aidan White *Humanitarian Aid 1/2003*

ETHICS

Munich Charter: Declaration of the rights and obligations of journalists 1971

ETHNIC CLEANSING

Kenan Malik *The Future 3/1997*
Wole Soyinka *November/December 1994*
WL Webb *Secret Chernobyls 1/1996*

EXILE

Wole Soyinka, Yang Lian, Gao Xingjian *Diaspora Voices 3/2002*

FATWA

Judith Moses *Post-Wall World November/December 1994*
Aziz Nesin *Fiction, Fact and the Fatwa* (Article 19, 1992)
Columbia journalism review *November 1994*
Taslima Nasrin *Publishing Now 2/1996*
Isioma Daniel *This Day* Nigeria November 2002

FILM

Philip French, Pauline Kael *November/December 1995*
Edward Lucie-Smith *The Full Cover Up 5/1998*
Anne Nelson *Tolerance and the Intolerable May/June 1994*
Julian Petley, Association of Chief Police Officers
    Media Moguls and Megalomania September/October 1994
Ken Loach *The Subversive Eye 6/1995*
Fiction, Fact and the Fatwa (Article 19, 1992)

FIRST AMENDMENT

Anthony Lewis *September/October 1995*
Peter Pringle *God is Not Dead 4/1996*

FREE EXPRESSION

Henry M Chakava *Publishing Now 2/1996*
Alina Vitukhnovskaya, Fyodor Dostoevsky *Art Unleashed 3/1996*
Fiction, Fact and the Fatwa (Article 19, 1992)
Bill Orme *Gagged for It 3/1998*
Stuart Hampshire *April 1992*
Ronald Dworkin *Tolerance and the Intolerable May/June 1994*
Ronald Dworkin *The Future 3/1997*

Ronald Dworkin *Filling the Silence 2/2002*
Anthony Lewis *UN: Make or Break 5/1995*
Phillip Knightley, Freimut Duve *Squeeze on Democracy 1/2002*
Yasar Kemal *1/1995*
Ivan Klíma *December 1981*
Salman Rushdie, *Fiction, Fact and the Fatwa* (Article 19, 1992)
Peter Porter and Harriet Harvey-Wood *Banned Poetry 5/1997*
Vitaly Tretyakov *This Sporting Life 4/2000*
Ronald Dworkin *Rewriting History 3/1995*

FREEDOM

Ivan Klíma *December 1981*
Peter Porter and Harriet Harvey Wood *Banned Poetry 5/1997*
Stephen Spender *Spring 1972*
Václav Havel, Shiva Kambari, Gore Vidal *Filling the Silence 2/2002*
Mark Fisher *Liberty in Britain 2/1995*

FREEDOM OF INFORMATION

Mark Fisher *Art Unleashed 3/1996*
Christopher Hird *Media Moguls and Megalomania September/October 1994*
Mark Fisher, Maurice Frankel *Liberty in Britain 2/1995*

GENOCIDE

Alex de Waal *Gagged for It 3/1998*
Slavenka Drakulic *Race Matters 3/2001*

GLOBALISATION

Leonardo Boff *The Last Empire 1/1999*
John Keane *Squeeze on Democracy 1/2002*

GOVERNMENT

Arthur Miller *May/June 1978*
Alan Clark *Liberty in Britain 2/1995*

HATE SPEECH

International Covenant on Civil and Political Rights Article 20, Ursula Owen,
   Aryeh Neier *Hate Speech 1/1998*
Richard Carver and Adewale Maja-Pearce *January/February 1995*
AL Kennedy *Filling the Silence 2/2002*
François Misser and Yves Jaumain *Media Moguls and Megalomania 4 & 5/1994*

HISTORY

Felipe Fernández-Armesto *Rewriting History 3/1995*
Michael Ignatieff *Wounded Nations, Broken Lives 5/1996*
WL Webb *Post-Wall World November/December 1994*
Urvashi Butalia, Amit Chaudhuri *Partitions 6/1997*
Stanley Cohen *Manufacturing Monsters 5/2000*
Nikita Khruschev, Isaac Deutscher, Eduardo Galeano, Baruch Kimmerling
   May/June 1995

HUMAN RIGHTS

European Convention on Human Rights 1/1966
John Searle *Art Unleashed 3/1996*
Caroline Moorehead *God is Not Dead 4/1996*
Caroline Moorehead and Ursula Owen *Secret Chernobyls 1/1996*
Caroline Moorehead, Ian Buruma, Caroline Moorehead *The Future 3/1997*

HUMOUR

Adam Phillips, Martin Rowson, Paul Krassner, Mark Twain, Saeed Okasha,
   Mark Nesbit, Roger Sabin, Art Spiegelman *The Last Laugh 6/2000*

IDENTITY

Amartya Sen *Filling the Silence 2/2002*
Mehmed Uzun *The Silence of Madness 4/2001*
Felipe Fernández-Armesto *May/June 1995*
Michael Ignatieff *Wounded Nations Broken Lives 5/1996*
Nicholas Fraser *Race Matters 3/2001*

KILLING

RSF *Annual Report 2002*
Ken Saro-Wiwa *Once and Future Shock 1/1996*
Caroline Moorehead *Tolerance and the Intolerable May/June 1994*
Vitaly Shentalinsky *8/1991*

LANGUAGE

Davrell Tien *Post-Wall World November/December 1994*
Ariel Dorfman, Rohan Jayasekera *The Privacy Issue 3/2000*
Ned Thomas *Identikit Europe 2/2001*
'In the News' *Women Who Censor 2/2000*
Yasar Kemal *January/February 1995*
Gao Xingjain *Diaspora Voices 3/2002*
Andrei Codrescu *September/October 1995*
Gill Newsham *Filling the Silence 2/2002*
Hugh Brody, Petrus Vaalboi *Tribes 1999*
Mehmed Uzun *The Silence of Madness 4/2001*

LAW

Noam Chomsky *The Future 3/1997*
Bill Orme *Gagged for It 3/1998*
Paul O'Connor *The Full Cover Up 5/1998*
Matthew D'Ancona *Tolerance and the Intolerable May/June 1994*
Hugh Stephenson *Partitions 6/1997*
Fabrice Rousselot, Philippa Nugent *Publishing Now 2/1996*
Godfrey Hodgson *Liberty in Britain 2/1995*
Helene Guldberg *Women Who Censor 2/2000*

LIBERTY

Mark Fisher *Liberty in Britain 2/1995*
Benjamin Franklin *Squeeze on Democracy 1/2002*

LIBRARIES

Luciano Canfora, William Golding, Lost libraries of the twentieth century (Selection)
   Word Power 2/1999

LIES

Elfriede Jelinek *Manufacturing Monsters 5/2000*
Dubravka Ugresic *Tolerance and the Intolerable May/June 1994*
Ursula Owen *Hate Speech 1/1998*
Ismaïl Kadare *Gagged for It 3/1998*

MADNESS

Adam Phillips, Sara Maitland, Danny Schechter *The Silence of Madness 4/2001*
Noam Chomsky *Manufacturing Monsters 5/2000*

MEDIA

Danny Schechter *Women Who Censor 2/2000*
Mark Thompson *After the Fall 5/1999*
Clive Hollick *Media Moguls and Megalomania September/October/1994*
Aryeh Neier *Hate Speech 1/1998*
Anthony Sampson *November/December 1991*
Wole Soyinka *November/December 1994*
Yasar Kemal *January/February 1995*
Nilou Mobasser, Roy Greenslade, Edward Said, Stanley Cohen
    Manufacturing Monsters 5/2000
Charles Glass *September/October 1996*
James D Squires *September/October 1995*
Maurice Frankel, Godfrey Hodgson *March/April 1995*
Václav Havel, Ronan Bennet *Filling the Silence 2/2002*
Philip Jones Griffiths *Underexposed 6/1999*
Rohan Jayasekera *Inside the Axis of Evil 1/2003*
Michael Grade *May/June 1994*
Laura Bruni *The Body Politic 4/1995*

MEMORY

Adam Phillips *Memory and Forgetting 1/2001*
Adam Phillips *Underexposed 6/1999*
Agusto Boal The *Last Empire 1/1999*
Jeremy Scott *Rewriting History 3/1995*
Dubravka Ugresic *Tolerance and the Intolerable May/June 1994*

Daikha Dridi, Gunter Grass, Frank Kermode, Stanley Cohen,
   Andrew Graham-Yooll *Memory and Forgetting 1/2001*
Birgit *Manufacturing Monsters 5/2000*
Judith Vidal-Hall *The Last Empire 1/1999*

MIGRATION

Campaign to Close Campsfield *Post-Wall World November/December 1994*
Citizen of Dover, Jeremy Hardy *Hate Speech 1/1998*
Roy Greenslade, Jeremy Harding *Manufacturing Monsters 5/2000*
Caroline Moorehead *Widows: Life After Death 2/1998*
Akash Kapur, Rohan Jayasekera *Diaspora Voices 3/2002*
Bob Sutcliffe *July/August 1994*
Irena Maryniak *The Future 3/1997*
Mehmed Uzun *The Silence of Madness 4/2001*

MINORITIES

Gara La Marche *UN: Make or Break 1995*
Vitaly Shentalinsky, Vitaly Shentalinsky *August/September 1991*
Yasar Kemal *Gay's the Word in Moscow 1/1995*
Edward Said *Gagged for It 3/1998*
Stephen Mulvey *Media Moguls & Media Megalomania September/October 1994*
Donald Kenrick *Liberty Knell July/August 1994*
Günter Grass *Gypsies: Life on the Edge 4/1998*

MULTICULTURALISM

Wolfgang Thierse *Race Matters 3/2001*
Michael Ignatieff *Filling the Silence 2/2002*
Kenan Malik *The Future 3/1997*
Marek Kohn *Big Science 3/1999*
Penelope Farmer *Liberty in Britain 2/1995*
Yasar Kemal *Gay's The Word in Moscow 1/1995*

MUSIC

Michael Tippett, Yehudi Menuhin *February 1983*
Martin Cloonan, Mark Ludwig, Gerald McBurney, Miles Marshall Lewis, Julien
   Petley, Mstislav Rostropovich *Smashed Hits 6/1998*

NATIONALISM

Edward Said *Gagged for Ît 3/1998*
Václav Havel, Salman Rushdie *The Future 3/1997*
Konstanty Gebert *After the Fall 5/1999*
Robert Fisk *The Full Cover Up 5/1998*

NUCLEAR POWER

Meir Vanunu, Mordechai Vanunu *April 1991*
Mikhail Byckau, David Hearst, Anthony Tucker *Secret Chernobyls 1/1996*
Noam Chomsky *Manufacturing Monsters 5/2000*
Tony Geraghty *Women Who Censor 2/2000*

OBSCENITY

Indian Penal Code, section 292
Soli J. Sorabjee, Colin Manchester *The Encyclopaedia of Censorship*
Amy Adler *Art Unleashed 3/1996*
Obscene Publications Act UK 1959
Lynne Walsh *Publishing Now 2/1996*

ORGANISATIONS

www.amnesty.org
www.article19.org
www.cpj.org
www.hrw.org
canada.ifex.org
www.indexonline.org
www.ifj.org
www.oneworld.org/internatpen
www.rsf.org

OWNERSHIP

Freimut Duve *Squeeze on Democracy 1/2002*
James D Squires *September/October 1995*
Rupert Murdoch, Leo Bogart *Media Moguls and Megalomania May/June 1994*
UK government White Paper *Liberty in Britain 2/1995*
Fabio Castillo *The New Slavery 1/2000*

James D Squires *September/October 1995*
Philip Jones Griffiths *Underexposed 6/1999*

PATRIOTISM

Anthony Lewis *September/October 1995*
Yasar Kemal *January/February 1995*
Arthur Miller *May/June 1978*
Yacov Guterman *Manufacturing Monsters 5/2000*
Dubravka Ugresic *May/June 1993*

PHOTOGRAPHY

Amy Adler *Art Unleashed 3/1996*
Philip Jones Griffiths *Partitions 6/1997*
Harold Evans *Underexposed 6/1999*

POLITICAL CORRECTNESS

Ursula Owen *Hate Speech 1/1998*
Anthony Lewis *September/October 1995*

PORNOGRAPHY

Elizabeth Wilson, British Board of Film Classification, Tuppy Owens, Lynne Segal
 Women Who Censor 2/2000
Erica Jong *July/August 1995*
Peter Brooks *Underexposed 6/1999*
Andrea Dworkin, Diana E Russell, quoted in *Women Who Censor 2/2000*

POVERTY

Mumia Abu-Jamal *1/1997 and 1/1999*
Mary Robinson, Neil Middleton *Gagged for It 3/1998*
James Gustave Speth *IHT 1996*

PRISON

PEN Writers in Prison *Tolerance and the Intolerable 1 and 2/1994*
Vitaly Shentalinsky on the USSR interviewed by Irena Maryniak
 August/September 1991
George Mangakis *1/1972*

PRIVACY

Lisa Forrell *Squeeze on Democracy 1/2002*
Simon Davies *The Privacy Issue 3/2000 and
    Race Matters 3/2001*
Privacy International Report 1995

PROPAGANDA

Santiago Kovadloff, Mark Thompson
    After the Fall 5/1999
David Miller 'The media: a user's manual' *July/August 1994*
George Conrad *Women Who Censor 2/2000*
A special correspondent *July/August 1995*
Danny Schechter *Underexposed 6/1999*
Mehmed Uzun *The Silence of Madness 4/2001*

QUEER

Gara Lamarche *Word Power 2/1999*
Alberto Manguel *Publishing Now 2/1996*
Lionel Blue, Alberto Manguel *Gay's The Word in Moscow 1/1995*
Scott Capurro *The Last Laugh 6/2000*

RACE

Marek Kohn *Big Science 3/1999*
Darryl Pinckney *God is Not Dead 4/1996*
Daniela Cestarollo, Primo Preto, Francisco Oliveira *The Last Empire 1/1999*
Anatolii Pristavkin, George Conrad *Women Who Censor 2/2000*
Kenan Malik *The Future 3/1997*
Ludvík Vakulík, Jeremy Hardy *Hate Speech 1/1998*
John Hoberman *This Sporting Life 4/2000*
Gara LaMarche *September/October 1995*
Nicola Lacey *Looking at Kids 2/1997*

RAPE

Naila Kabeer *The Body Politic 4/1995*
Umberto Eco *Tolerance and the Intolerable 1 and 2/1994*
Valerie Ceccherini, Pakistani woman *The Last Empire 1/1999*

READING

Alberto Manguel *Gay's The Word in Moscow 1/1995*
Alberto Manguel and Craig Stephenson *Lost Words 6/1996*

RELIGION

UN Universal Declaration of Human Rights Article 18
Valerie Ceccherini, Leonardo Boff *The Last Empire 1/1999*
Felipe Fernandez-Armesto *Memory and Forgetting 1/2001*
George Konrad *Women Who Censor 2/2000*
Urvashi Butalia *Partitions 6/1997*
Stuart Hampshire *April 1992*
Sidharth Bhatia, Abdol Karim Soroush *Squeeze on Democracy 1/2002*
Darryl Pinckney, Baruch Kimmerling *God is Not Dead 4/1996*
Irena Maryniak *God is Not Dead 4/1996 and After the Fall 5/1999*

SAMIZDAT

Yuri Andropov *Rewriting History 3/1995*
Larisa Bogoraz, Geoffrey Hosking
   Filling the Silence 2/2002
Dietrich A Loeber *Autumn 1973*

SCIENCE

Colin Tudge, Gregory Palast *Big Science 3/1999*

SECRECY

Vitaly Shentalinsky *August/September 1991*
Vera Rich *Big Science 3/1999*
Judith Vidal-Hall *Publishing Now 2/1996*
Gore Vidal *Filling the Silence 2/2002*
Meir Vanunu *10/1991*
Michael Grade *Tolerance and the Intolerable*
   1 and 2/1994

SEX

Broadcasting Standards Commission, Julian Petley *The New Slavery 1/2000*
Urvashi Butalia, Lynne Walsh *Publishing Now 2/1996*

SILENCING

Sara Maitland *The Silence of Madness 4/2001*
Kim Normanton, Stembiso, Irena Maryniak *Women Who Censor 2/2000*
Yossi *Manufacturing Monsters 5/2000*
Zoran Filipovic *UN: Make or Break 5/1995*
Tom Stoppard *December 1981*

SLAVERY

Urvashi Butalia, Vassudha Daghamvar *Looking at Kids 2/1997*
Kevin Bales and Humfrey Hunter, Ali Hassan, Harry Wu, Alan Hope,
    Bob Sutcliffe *The New Slavery 1/2000*

TECHNOLOGY

British Medical Association 1999
Arthur C Clarke *November/December 1995*
Chris Ellison *After the Fall 5/1999*
Christopher Hird *Media Moguls and Megalomania 4 and 5/1994*

TERRORISM

Michael Ignatieff, Gore Vidal *Filling the Silence 2/2002*
Judith Vidal-Hall *The Silence of Madness 4/2001*
Nadine Strossen *September/October 1995*
Claire Fauset *Race Matters 3/2001*
Mark Fisher, Mark Pedelty, Pervez Hoodbhoy, Freimut Duve
    Squeeze on Democracy 1/2002
Frank Fisher *The New Slavery 1/2000*

TOLERANCE

Umberto Eco *Tolerance & the Intolerable May/June 1994*
Fiction, Fact and the Fatwa (Article 19, 1992)
Ronald Dworkin, Ariel Dorman *The Future 3/1997*

TORTURE

Agusto Boal *The Last Empire 1/1999*
Eduardo Galeano *March/April 1978*

Ursula Owen *Squeeze on Democracy 1/2002*
Khmer Rouge S21 Interrogator's manual 1986

TRANSLATION

Richard McKane *Diaspora Voices 3/2002*
Alberto Manguel *Publishing Now 2/1996*
Fiction, Fact and the Fatwa (Article 19, 1992)

TRUTH & RECONCILIATION

Judge Goldstone on War Crimes Tribunals *May/June 1995*
Universal Declaration of Human Rights *Gagged for It 3/98*
Vitaly Shentalinsky *August/September 1991*
Stanley Cohen *Manufacturing Monsters 5/2000*
Pieter-Dirk Uys, Michael Ignatieff, Nelson Mandela, FW De Klerk,
    Ntsiki Biko, Desmond Tutu *Wounded Nations Broken Lives 5/1996*
Umberto Eco *Tolerance and the Intolerable 1 and 2/1994*

UNITED NATIONS

Abdullah al Udhari *Gagged for It 3/1998*
Robert Maharaj *Post-Wall World November/December 1994*
Damir, David Rieff, Semsa, Michael Ignatieff, Tadeusz Mazowiecki
    UN: Make or Break 5/1995

UNIVERSAL DECLARATION OF HUMAN RIGHTS

Alex de Waal, Bill Orme, Michael Ignatieff, Aryeh Neier, Martin Simecka,
    Konstanty Gebert , Noam Chomsky, Mary Robinson *Gagged for It 3/1998*
Abdullahi An-Na'im *Media Moguls and Megalomania 4 and 5/1994*

URL

Natasha Schmidt *The Privacy Issue 3/2000*

VIOLENCE

Naila Kabeer,Caroline Moorehead *The Body Politic 4/1995*
Yasmin Alibhai-Brown, Irena Maryniak *Women Who Censor 2/2000*
Aung San Suu Kyi *The Future 3/1997*

WAR

Ronald Dworkin *Filling the Silence 2/2002*
Phillip Knightley, Matthew D'Ancona *April/May 1991*
Juan Goytisolo *Wounded Nations Broken Lives 5/1996*
Mark Pedelty *Squeeze on Democracy 1/2002*
Alex de Waal *After the Fall 5/1999*

WHISTLEBLOWERS

Maurice Frankel *March/April 1995*
AL Kennedy *Filling the Silence 2/2002*

WOMEN

Abdul Bari-Atwan *God is Not Dead 4/1996*
Jesse Banfield *The Future 3/1997*
Caroline Moorehead *Widows: Life After Death 2/1998*
Elizabeth Wilson *Women Who Censor 2/2002*
Shere Hite *July/August 1994*
Mary Kenny *Manufacturing Monsters 5/2000*
Naila Kabeer, Laura Bruni and Nevine Mabro
    July/August 1995
Rizia Begum *Gagged for It 3/98*
Caroline Moorehead, Naila Kabeer
    The Body Politic 4/1995
Alan Hope *The New Slavery 1/2000*

WORDS

Anthony Lewis *UN: Make or Break 5/1995*
Stephen Spender *The Body Politic 4/1995*
Eduardo Galeano *March/April 1978*
Václav Havel *November/December 1986*
Goenawan Mohamad *Looking at Kids 2/1997*
Alberto Manguel and Craig Stephenson *Lost Words 6/1996*
Amanda Romero *The New Slavery 1/2000*

WRITERS

Stephen Spender *Tolerance and the Intolerable May/June 1994*
Vitaly Shentalinsky *August/September 1991*
Alexandr Zinovev, Irena Maryniak *Publishing Now 2/1996*
Salman Rushdie *March/April 1996* and *The Future 3/1997*
Joseph Brodsky *Autumn/Winter 1972*
Satyavathi, AL Kennedy *Filling the Silence 2/2002*
Nadine Gordimer *Summer 1976*
Arthur Miller *May/June 1978*
Gao Xingjian, Yang Lian *Diaspora Voices 3/2002*
Alexander Solzhenitsyn *2/1972*
Alberto Manguel and Craig Stephenson *Lost Words 6/1996*

XENOPHOBIA

Michael Ignatieff *Filling the Silence 2/2002*
Elfriede Jelinek *Manufacturing Monsters 5/2000*
Norman Stone *Identikit Europe 2/2001*

XINGXING

Desmond A Skeel *Censorship: A World Encyclopaedia*

YOUR POCKET GUIDE TO SEX

Martin Cloonan *Censorship: A World Encyclopaedia*

Z

Michael Griffin *Race Matters 3/2001*

Index of contributors